STUDIES IN MODERN GREEK

C.P. Cavafy

Studies in Modern Greek

The Greek Folk Songs, Niki Watts (1988)

C.P. Cavafy, Christopher Robinson (1988)

Nikos Kazantzakis—Novelist, Peter Bien (1989)

Solomos, Peter Mackridge (1989)

The Development of the Greek Language, Wendy Moleas (1989)

Erotokritos, David Holton (1990)

Seferis, Roderick Beaton (1990)

STUDIES IN MODERN GREEK

C. P. CAVAFY

CHRISTOPHER ROBINSON

BRISTOL CLASSICAL PRESS U.K.
ARISTIDE D. CARATZAS, PUBLISHER U.S.A.

First published in 1988 by:

U.K.	U.S.A.
Bristol Classical Press	Aristide D. Caratzas
226 North Street	P.O. Box 210
Bedminster	481 Main Street
Bristol BS3 1JD	New Rochelle
	NY 10802

ISBN 1-85399-034-5   ISBN 0-89241-469-3 (Hbk)
0-89241-470-7 (Pbk)

The assistance of the London Hellenic Society is gratefully acknowledged.

Printed and bound in Great Britain by
Short Run Press Ltd., Exeter

For my wife Carole

SERIES PREFACE

This new series of critical studies will make the findings of the considerable research into Modern Greek literature available in a form and at a level accessible to the student, the teacher and the general reader.

These introductory books should be invaluable to those seeking an understanding of, and a critical guide to, the study of some of the most widely read figures of Modern Greek literature. It has been specifically designed to cater for the needs of those studying for GCE 'A' level Modern Greek in the UK and undergraduates in the UK, Australia and the USA.

The major concerns of each author are examined critically and objectively, and the background, style and language as well as characterisation, where relevant, of the works are discussed.

Special thanks are due to the Standing Committee of Modern Greek in the Universities (SCOMGIU) in the UK for their support of the series from its inception, and to Bristol Classical Press for making its realisation possible.

Niki Watts
Series Editor

Η νέα αυτή σειρά κριτικών θα κάνει τα ευρήματα της σημαντικής έρευνας που διεξάγεται στον τομέα της σύγχρονης Ελληνικής λογοτεχνίας διαθέσιμα σε μια μορφή και ένα επίπεδο προσιτό στο φοιτητή, το δάσκαλο και το γενικό αναγνώστη.

Τα εισαγωγικά αυτά βιβλία θα είναι χρήσιμα για όσους επιθυμούν να μελετήσουν μερικά από τα πιο πολυδιαβασμένα συγγράμματα της σύγχρονης Ελληνικής λογοτεχνίας και αναζητούν έναν κριτικό οδηγό. Έχουν δε σχεδιαστεί με σκοπό να ανταποκρίνονται ιδιαίτερα στις απαιτήσεις όσων μελετούν Νεοελληνική φιλολογία για τις εξετάσεις GCE 'Α' level στην Αγγλία καθώς και των φοιτητών των Νεοελληνικών σε πανεπιστήμια της Αγγλίας, Αυστραλίας και των Ηνωμένων Πολιτειών Αμερικής.

Οι σημαντικότερες επιδιώξεις του κάθε συγγραφέα εξετάζονται κριτικά και αντικειμενικά και συζητούνται η γλώσσα, οι ιδέες και οι χαρακτήρες των έργων.

Θα ήθελα να ευχαριστήσω ιδιαιτέρως την Επιτροπή για τη Διδασκαλία των Νέων Ελληνικών στα Αγγλικά Πανεπιστήμια (SCOMGIU) για την υποστήριξή της, ηθική και έμπρακτη, καθώς και τον εκδοτικό οίκο Bristol Classical Press που ανέλαβε την έκδοση της σειράς.

Νίκη Watts
Εκδοτική επιμέλεια

CONTENTS

	Page
PART I: Content or tone of voice?	1
1. The influence of the Decadents	2
2. The erotic themes	7
3. The historical themes	9
4. Irony	11
5. The voices in Cavafy's poetry	21
PART II: Poetic technique	31
1. Rhythm	31
2. Sound patterning	36
2.1 rhyme	36
2.2. other forms of sound patterning	42
3. Language	44
3.1 word order	46
3.2 choice and stylisation of vocabulary	48
3.3. register	55
4. Structural patterning	60
PART III: Eight commentaries	64
1. Εν απογνώσει	65
2. Μέσα στα καπηλειά	70
3. Ενας νέος, της Τέχνης του Λόγου - στο 24ον έτος του	75
4. Καισαρίων	81
5. Εν Σπάρτη	87
6. Η μάχη της Μαγνησίας	92
7. Φιλέλλην	97
8. Μύρης· Αλεξάνδρεια του 340 μX.	101

BIBLIOGRAPHY

1. Text

K.P. Kavafis; Ποιήματα 2 vols. ed. G. Savidis (Ikaros, Athens 1965)

2. Translations

The Complete Poems of C.P. Cavafy trans. Rae Dalven, intro. by W.H. Auden (Hogarth Press, London 1961)

C.P. Cavafy: Collected Poems ed. G. Savidis, trans. E. Keeley and P. Sherrard (Princeton and London 1975)

3. Secondary literature

(All works in this section are suitable for use by teachers and university students, but only those marked with an asterisk are likely to be comprehensible to younger students.)

Biography
* R. Liddell *Cavafy* (Duckworth, London 1974)

Criticism: a) books
* P. Bien *Constantine Cavafy* (Columbia Essays on Modern Writers) (New York 1964)
* C.M. Bowra *The Creative Experiment* (Macmillan, London 1967)
* E. Keeley *Cavafy's Alexandria* (Hogarth Press, London 1977)
* E. Keeley 'Voice, Perspective and Context in Cavafy' in *Modern Greek Poetry, Voice and Myth* (Princeton, New Jersey 1983)

Κύκλος Καβάφη Athens 1983 (papers given at the Εταιρεία Σπουδών Νεοελληνικού Πολιτισμού και Γενικής Παιδείας, Ίδρυμα Σχολής Μωραΐτη)

Κ. Μήνας *Η Γλώσσα του Καβάφη* (University of Jannina, 1985)

P.M. Minucci *Kavafis* (La Nuova Italia, Florence 1979)

Ι.Μ. Παναγιωτόπουλος *Πρόσωπα και κείμενα* vol.4 (Athens 1946)

M. Peri *Quattro saggi su Kavafis* (Pubblicazioni della Universita Cattolica, Milan 1977)

* N. Vayenas 'The Language of Irony' in *The Mind and Art of C.P. Cavafy: Essays on his Life and Work* ed. Denise Harvey (Denise Harvey and Co. Athens 1983)

Criticism: b) articles

M. Alexiou 'Eroticism and Poetry' *Journal of the Hellenic Diaspora* X (1983) 45-65

R. Beaton 'C.P. Cavafy: Irony and Hellenism' *The Slavonic and East European Review* vol.59 (1981) 516-528

R. Beaton 'The History Man' *Journal of the Hellenic Diaspora* X (1983) 23-44

ACKNOWLEDGEMENTS

Although this book will (I hope) constitute an original contribution to the study of Cavafy, I have of course drawn heavily on other published criticism of his poems. In view of the sort of readership to which the book is primarily directed, it seemed more appropriate, rather than fill the text with footnotes marking my sources, to acknowledge a general debt to the works listed in my bibliography and a considerable particular debt to the work of Massimo Peri, without which much of parts two and three of this book would never have taken shape.

PART I: CONTENT OR TONE OF VOICE?

Cavafy is a poet whose life throws little light on his poems. Apart from the periods spent, during his youth, in England and in Constantinople, he hardly left Alexandria, where he led an uneventful existence marked only by occasional family dramas and the dull routine of a minor post in the Irrigation Office. Even his statements about his own writing are not always helpful. He declared, for example, that his poems could be divided into three categories: philosophical, historical and erotic. Yet such a division is positively misleading if we take it literally. Many of the poems are plainly both historical and erotic, and only a handful of poems are overtly philosophical (most of these being about ethical questions), whereas many more poems have philosophical implications.

Another unhelpful statement is the remark attributed to him, that, while many other poets were just poets, he was a historian-poet. The term ποιητής ιστορικός tells us no more than that he saw the historical element in his subject matter as of great importance. The writing of history is an art which has undergone constant development: there is no such thing as a historian's attitude to life. The past means different things to different historians. Nor does Cavafy use a historian's methodology in his approach to the past. As his biographer Robert Liddell has pointed out, Cavafy seldom reveals a historian's view of cause and effect. His fascination with the past is a fascination with individual personal moments, with the clash of different ways of viewing a single moment, and with types, moods, experiences which seem to transcend time. It is the fascination of an artist, not of a historian.

1

1. The influence of the Decadents

But if Cavafy's biography and his literary theory give us little help in understanding his poetry, an appreciation of the artistic context of his writing does help us to some extent. Although many critics have stressed how separate Cavafy is from both the European and Greek poetic traditions of his day, we shall approach his poetry more perceptively if we see it as deeply rooted in the French literary movement of the 1870s and '80s known as Decadence. This is a very technical term, with no moral connotations.

The work of the Decadents, notably the novel *Against Nature* by J–K. Huysmans and the poetry of Jules Laforgue, defined a modern sensibility, as the writers of the period conceived of it. These writers saw no reason to believe in God or in any permanent values at all. To them, life consisted of fragmented experiences and sensations which held significance only for the individuals experiencing them. Therefore individual emotional responses to intense experiences became the most important things in life. But there is often a sense of Fate in their work too. For, though time is experienced as a disconnected set of isolated moments, it is also an inexorable movement towards death. The individual is trapped in the fated onward sweep towards annihilation. Only art stood some chance of creating meaning out of the pointlessness of everyday existence.

Whether or not Cavafy actually read any of the relevant French writers is not important. Much French and English prose and poetry of the last decades of the nineteenth century was influenced by their attitudes. If he was attracted to their way of seeing the world, he could hardly have avoided coming across its literary expression in one or more of the languages which he could read. But we do have one piece of concrete evidence of the way in which Cavafy shared attitudes with the Decadents. Like them he read the poems *Les fleurs du mal* by the slightly earlier French poet Charles Baudelaire (1821-67), the writer generally seen as the father of modern European poetry, and like them he was particularly attracted by Baudelaire's idea that human experience is

The influence of the Decadents

characteristically made up of stretches of mindless monotony broken by brief but intense sensations which momentarily bring us to life. We see this very clearly in an unpublished poem by Cavafy (dated August 1891) called 'Ἀλληλουχία κατά τον Βωδελαίρον'. Into this poem Cavafy works a translation of the whole of Baudelaire's poem 'Correspondences', in which he explores the artist's ability to see beyond the superficial meaning of physical reality. Cavafy then restates the idea that poets have superior powers of perception, and adds a further ten lines of his own on the fragmented nature of other men's experience, emphasising the elements of sensations and emotion (αἴσθησις, νοσταλγία, ρίγος, χαρά, εν τη καρδία), chance (τυχαίας, αναίτιος) and brevity (εφήμερος, σύντομος, βραχεία, μιας στιγμής, αιφνιδίως (twice)):

> Εν παραδείσω σκοτεινώ οι άνθρωποι
> οι άλλοι ψηλαφώσι δρόμον χαλεπόν.
> Κ' η μόνη λάμψις ήτις κάποτ' ως σπινθήρ
> εφήμερος φωτίζει της πορείας των
> την νύκτα, είναι σύντομός τις αίσθησις
> μαγνητικής τυχαίας γειτνιάσεως—
> βραχεία νοσταλγία, ρίγος μιάς στιγμής,
> όνειρον ώρας της ανατολής, χαρά
> αναίτιός τις αιφνιδίως ρέουσα
> εν τη καρδία κ' αιφνιδίως φεύγουσα.

In his own later work, this will be the picture not just of man in general, but of the poet himself as a representative man. He will no longer present the poet as perceiving more but as having the power to transcend the fleetingness of the intense moments by preserving them in art.

If I am right in claiming that Cavafy's poetry has its roots in the work of the Decadents, then the affinity should be clear from the early published works onwards. We should be aware of the central importance of experiencing each present moment, the threat of being stifled by the

3

meaninglessness and boredom of everyday routine, passivity in the face of the outside world and a feeling of the impossibility of communicating with others. Actions should seem to be valid simply because people decide to commit them, not because they express some accepted absolute value. And art should be seen as the only thing creating meaning in, and out of, life. As we shall see, all these elements are indeed present.

The early poems are usually interpreted in a very 'moral' way, and they do have a decidedly didactic tone which seems to justify such as interpretation. But the view of the world which they contain is not as stable and conventional as their form might suggest. Take 'Ἰθάκη' and 'Ἡ πόλις', for example. At first sight 'Ithaca' is an elaboration on the maxim 'it is better to travel hopefully than to arrive'. It does admittedly suggest that there are attainable absolutes such as wisdom, something no Decadent would accept. But the poem is principally a call to get as much as you can out of whatever experience life offers you. And that experience is defined in sensual terms, not intellectual ones: the pleasure of entering a port for the first time (i.e. undergoing any new experience), the purchase of mother-of-pearl and coral, amber and ebony. The sense stressed is the least cerebral of all the senses, that of smell:

καὶ ἡδονικά μυρωδικά κάθε λογῆς,
ὅσο μπορεῖς πιό ἄφθονα ἡδονικά μυρωδικά

and the repeated adjective describing the perfume, ἡδονικά, links their sensuality to sexuality.

'Ἰθάκη' is a poem about giving in to the intense pleasure of the moment: it raises the idea to the status of a purpose in life. 'Ἡ πόλις', though a more obviously moralising poem, is in a sense merely the same theme viewed in reverse. It contains an elaboration of the idea summed up by the Roman poet Horace: 'Caelum non animum mutant qui trans mare currunt' (Those who rush off across the sea change their physical horizons but not their mental ones). This might seem directly to contradict the value ascribed to new experience in 'Ἰθάκη'. But the difference is not one of experience, but of attitude to experience. The addressee of 'Η πόλις' sees life in a certain way and will therefore always experience it in that way. Unlike the potential traveller of 'Ιθάκη' he is not open to the joys of the present. He is trapped between pointless hope for the future and pointless regret for the past. Thus the two poems together offer a view of the self which not only accords with the Decadent insistence on the overwhelming importance of the present, but also goes on to give importance to the idea of constantly renewed action, with the proviso that you must approach each new experience with an open mind. Cavafy is here a forerunner of the twentieth century Existentialist movement, which believes that we create ourselves by our own actions.

What the protagonist of 'Η πόλις' has given in to is the sense of the pointlessness of all human activity which haunts Baudelaire and the Decadents—Κάθε προσπάθεια μου μια καταδίκη είναι γραφτή—and the loss of emotional capacity which this brings—κ' είν' η καρδιά μου—σαν νεκρός—θαμένη. These are symptoms of what the nineteenth-century French writers called *ennui*, a complete weariness with life which haunts their poems and has, of course, its most explicit expression, in the work of Cavafy, in the poems 'Μονοτονία':

Και καταντά το αύριο πιά σαν αύριο να μη μοιάζει

and 'Στο πλητικό Χωριό'. When time ceases to be a series of distinct, intense moments and becomes a relentless, oppressive continuum, the poet relapses into the condition of the ordinary man, trapped in the race towards death. The image of entrapment is more specifically present in 'Τείχη', with its sense of inexorable exclusion from communication with the world around one and of consequent isolation in the self. But we find a related and perhaps more interesting manifestation of the effects of ennui in the passivity which characterises the citizens in 'Περιμένοντας τους βαρβάρους'. Here all hope for a release from the routine of life is placed on an outside force, the barbarians, whose existence is then placed in doubt. Pleasure may be best, but pain is

5

preferable to numbness: better to fall victim to an outside force than to linger on in meaninglessness. Even those poems which appear to support more conventional values may be misleading. Take heroism, for example. Critics of Cavafy are sometimes puzzled by poems which appear to promote admiration of self-sacrifice of a rather Stoical sort, e.g. 'Θερμοπύλες', 'Che fece ... il gran rifiuto', ''Αγε ώ βασιλεύ Λακεδαιμονίων'. But are these poems really about heroism (let alone patriotism in a conventional sense)? Take 'Θερμοπύλες'. The first stanza does indeed praise conventional values, but the second adds more than just the idea that it is more heroic to face a danger in full consciousness of the risks. It introduces the idea of an action done for the sake of it, in full knowledge of its ultimate pointlessness. Cavafy holds up defenders of hopeless positions (symbolised by Thermopylae) for our admiration, because of the arbitrary stubbornness of the roles they choose to play. In a pointless world, a heroic role is merely a more positive role to play than an unheroic one. Cratisicleia, the Spartan queen in ''Αγε ώ βασιλεύ Λακεδαιμονίων', is treated in much the same way. These people give themselves a meaning by their adoption of a heroic role. But this does not mean that the poet is praising conventional heroism as such.

I do not want to overstate my case. Of course there are, in the early poems of Cavafy, moralising elements and moral stances which have nothing to do with the world-view of the Decadents, and no bearing on the themes of fragmentation of time, intensity of ephemeral experience, instability of values, monotony and passivity which the Greek poet shared with his French predecessors. But the tendency to read the early poems as a set of morally improving maxims, even if some of Cavafy's own statements about them support such readings, is a reductive one, which disguises the connection between these poems and Cavafy's later ones. Very well, you may say, suppose that we accept that these elements are present in Cavafy's poems. How do they fit with the major thematic elements which critics identify in the later works: the erotic and the historical?

2. The erotic themes

Let us consider the case of the erotic themes first. Homosexuality is, of course, a frequent feature of the lives and writings of French and English Decadents (e.g. Paul Verlaine, Oscar Wilde). But the erotic themes of Cavafy's poetry, whether presented in a historical or a modern setting, are linked in more significant ways to the world-view we have already been discussing. As the English poet W.H. Auden has aptly observed: 'The erotic world he depicts is one of casual pick-ups and short-lived affairs'. Such moments of chance sensual pleasure are at their briefest in such poems as 'Η προθήκη του καπνοπωλείου' and 'Μια νύχτα'. They may record responses as much aesthetic as sensual, as in 'Στου καφενείου την είσοδο'. And indeed an important group link fleeting physical encounters very specifically to the lasting nature of the art which records them, expounding the distinctly Baudelairean and Decadent thesis that life receives its meaning and justification in the stimulation it gives to the artist's creative faculties. A good example of such a poem is 'Να μείνει', with its extended dramatic evocation of a moment of the swiftest and most basic sexual fulfilment and its observation of how that experience

                    ... τώρα ήλθε
    να μείνει μες στην ποίησιν αυτή.

Cavafy does indeed portray sensuality as a fragmented, fleeting impetus to art, at least when filtered through the transforming power of memory, and in 'Ίμενος' for example, lays great stress on the intensity of such experiences. But even here the link to the decadent world-view is broader and more interesting than may be obvious at first glance. For Cavafy's presentation of sexuality is part of his wider presentation of changeability and instability, and it is here that his poems on 'personal' themes and on 'political' ones most obviously meet.

The poet may have chosen to concentrate exclusively on homosexuality because of his own temperament, but as Marcel Proust also

7

discovered, homosexual love, because it lacks the artificial stabilising factors provided by social institutions such as marriage, casts a crueller light on problems of human relationship which are also relevant to heterosexuality. Love, in Cavafy, is at the mercy of poverty, greed, chance and above all death. It usually succumbs to them.

It is noticeable that the poet focusses on love-affairs at their moments of greatest instability—when one of the lovers is obsessed by fear of abandonment ('Δύο νέοι, 23 έως 24 ετών'), is trying to cope with having been abandoned ('Το 25ον έτος του βίου του') or with an inequality of passion ('Ενας νέος, της Τέχνης του Λόγου—στο 24ον έτος του'), or where separation is forced on the couple by circumstances ('Πριν τους αλλάξει ο Χρόνος'). The nuances of emotional complexity can be very subtle, as in 'Κίμων Λεάρχου', where the sense of loss at the death of a friend and cousin is complicated by the fact that the cousin had previously stolen the speaker's lover.

No two poems ever quite cover the same ground. Thus abandonment, treated in both 'Μέσα στα καπήλεια' and 'Το 25ον έτος του βίου του', is seen in terms of its long-term effects on the abandoned lover in the former poem, and the refusal of the abandoned lover to accept the realities of the situation in the latter. This fascination with the nuances of unsettled characters and unstable situations extends well beyond the erotic poems. It is a feature of poems which show characters caught between two opposing tendencies or desires in themselves, such as Myrtias ('Τα επικίνδυνα'), who believes that he can switch at will from sensuality to asceticism—the title of the poem undermines his claim— or Ianthis ('Των Εβραίων (50 M.X.)'), who wrongly believes that he can reject hedonistic Hellenism and become a devout Jew. There is nothing accidental about this recurrence of themes of changeability, and of the relativity of all human values and feelings which this changeability reveals. It is at the heart of what attracts Cavafy to his subject matter. A passage from his so-called 'Ars poetica' (Art of poetry), an essay written in English in 1903, shows that he was conscious of the fact himself:

"Also care should be taken not to lose from sight that a state of feeling is true or false, possible and impossible at the same time, or rather by turns. And the poet—who even when he works most philosophically, remains an artist—gives one side, which does not mean that he denies the other [...] He merely describes a possible and an occurring state of feeling—sometimes very transient, sometimes of some duration."

This changeability of the feelings and values of the poet himself he has learnt, in his mature poetry, to project onto the multiplicity of characters who people his poems.

3. The historical themes

Here, then is the link to the historical poetry proper (by which I mean the poetry which draws attention to particular events and periods in history, as opposed to the erotic poems with historical settings). The instability of individual lives is reflected in the destabilisation of social institutions at given political moments. Stability in politics, like heroism in battle, creates an illusion of apparently permanent meaning: disintegration and defeat reveal the multiplicity of human reactions to adversity and the relativity of all human activity. Hence Cavafy's preference for the world of Ptolemaic Egypt, of the courts of the Seleucid kings, of the Greek-speaking world under the rule of Rome. Hence his taste for politically ambiguous moments—such as the outcome of the battle of Actium ('Εν δήμω της Μικράς Ασίας, Το 31 Π.Χ στην Αλεξάνδρεια)—and for attitudes adopted by a character in good faith but destined to be proved wrong by contemporary events or the later course of history ('Εν πορεία προς την Σινώπην, Στα 200 Π.Χ.'). Hence his interest in shifts from paganism to Christianity and vice versa ('Θέατρον της Σιδώνος', 'Μύρης, Αλεξάνδρεια του 340 Μ.Χ.', and the poems about the emperor Julian). That is why, though there are clear personal and

9

cultural reasons for Cavafy's interest in Alexandria and the Greek East in general, it seems to me a mistake to view his treatment of Alexandria in particular, and of Greece in the Hellenistic and Roman periods in general, as a historically-based investigation of the rise and fall of a particular facet of Greek civilisation, let alone as a symbol of Cavafy's own passage from growth and vigour to old age and failing powers, as Peter Bien does in his short study of the poet:

> "Just as he himself had enjoyed youth and vigour only to watch them give way inexorably to decrepitude, so the various Hellenistic centres had undergone the same process, and the method by which he could recapture in poetry the soars and swoops of his own history was to evoke, in all its facets, the history of his race— and in particular, the vicissitudes of that race in Alexandria."

The 'history' which Cavafy presents is not a sequential study of the type which this interpretation implies. On the contrary, Cavafy sees time as a series of disconnected moments, not as a coherent pattern. Like later European writers, though in a less systematic and philosophical way, Cavafy is exploring the paradox of how a sense of human continuity can exist despite the apparent disconnection and fragmentation both of individual perception and experience and of social institutions and historical processes.

I would go so far as to say that Cavafy should not primarily be read for his 'content' at all. What he has to say about time, memory, beauty, sensuality, art, religion, political power etc. is of course of interest. But it is not a poetry of fixed meaning in the way that such words as 'content' or 'subject matter' would seem to imply. That side of 'meaning' he leaves to his readers to create for themselves from their individual response to a poem or group of poems. As he puts it in another passage of his 'Ars poetica': "Very often the poet's work has but a vague meaning: it is a suggestion ...". The subject matter has all been filtered through a world-view which has helped the poet to formulate his poetic manner. Consequently, the reader must be as attentive to *how* things are said as to what is said. The next problem, then, is how to identify this 'poetic manner'. W.H. Auden (who could not read Modern Greek) found himself at a loss to explain what it was in Cavafy that survives translation into English, and came to the conclusion that it was "Something I can only call, most inadequately, a tone of voice, a personal speech". A key feature in defining this attitude, this 'tone of voice', is the complex question of irony.

4. Irony

In several of his earlier poems Cavafy takes the ironies of history as his subject matter. His standard method is to describe the way in which a historical character, real or imaginary, sees the world, and then to describe the future events which will disprove or overthrow that view of the world. His two poems about the Roman emperor Nero, 'Τα βήματα' and 'Η διορία του Νέρωνος', are a good example of the way in which he develops the technique of doing this. 'Τα βήματα' (written in the period 1893-1908) is barely ironic at all. In it Cavafy paints a brief picture of Nero, showing his love of pleasure and luxury but emphasising his calm and ease: he is sleeping, he is peaceful, he is happy. The greater part of the poem is then taken up with a description of how the household gods are nervous at the sound of the approaching steps of the Furies. The dramatic irony of the situation is merely suggested, and the only linguistic irony is the adjective ασυνείδητος: Nero in his deep sleep is unaware of the world around him, but he is also, as the second half of the poem suggests, unaware of his approaching doom.

'Η διορία του Νέρωνος' approaches its subject in a less didactic manner. Cavafy seems to have learnt the technique from the French Parnassian poets. Instead of describing the Emperor's psychological state from the outside in an abstract way, Cavafy takes an incident from Suetonius' *Life of Nero*. Nero consults the Delphic oracle and is advised

11

to 'fear the 73 years'. The first two stanzas (three-quarters of the poem)
describe Nero's reaction to the oracle from inside, using a technique
called 'free indirect speech'. In the first three lines an impersonal
narrator tells us that Nero was not worried by the oracle. In the fourth
line, the statement

Εἶχε καιρόν ἀκόμη νὰ χαρεῖ

could be the voice of the same narrator, or a representation of Nero's
inner thoughts: [he thought that] he still had time to enjoy himself. The
latter interpretation fits well with the tense shift which follows. In l.5 the
poem moves into the present tense, and remains there till the end. Lines
5-13 are clearly Nero's own view of the world. This is particularly
noticeable in lines 11-13, where the poem becomes a series of broken
reflections on the physical pleasures of the emperor's travels in Greece,
culminating in the exclamation

Α των γυμνών σωμάτων η ηδονή προ πάντων ...

Then, tacked on in a short three-line stanza, is the event that Nero is
unaware of. The future emperor Galba is secretly training troops in
Spain to overthrow Nero. The present tense in this last stanza is not the
tense of Nero's thoughts but a dramatic present, stressing the fact that
these events occur *while* Nero is happily reflecting on the pleasures of
life. We are left to see the irony for ourselves, but it is still explicit, for
Cavafy spells out for us in the final line that Galba is seventy-three years
old.

In 'Η διορία του Νέρωνος' Cavafy uses a familiar historical event
to create his dramatic irony. In another poem written in the same year,
'Πρέσβεις απ' την Αλεξάνδρεια', we find a comparable dramatic
structure, though the role of the inner voice is much reduced. This time
we are dealing with an event in Egyptian history, the quarrel between
Ptolemy VI Philometor and his younger brother Ptolemy VIII

Euergetes II as to who should rule. The quarrel was resolved when Philometor was restored to the throne by the Romans in 163 B.C. Cavafy has invented (apparently) an application by the two brothers to the Delphic oracle to know who will be the victor in the disagreement. Cavafy was evidently attracted by the ambiguous answers for which the oracle was famous and which were often associated with mistaken expectations of the future on the part of the person consulting the oracle. But here Cavafy does not rely for the focus of the irony on the historical characters. The poem focusses instead on the dilemma of the priests: how are they to create an oracle ambiguous enough to take in two opposing powerful figures? The irony lies in the irrelevance of the priests' activities. The issue is not a religious but a political one, and as such is solved by the supreme political force of the day, the Romans. In the metaphorical phrase

Στην Ρώμη δόθηκε ο χρησμός

the poem emphasises the transfer of power from Apollo to the Romans, from the divine sphere to the human one. But there is a double irony. For, at the same time, the poem shows that the power always did lie in the human sphere, since the priests were always ignorant, the oracle was never more than a trick. In that sense the use of irony in the poem is slightly more elaborate than that in 'Η διορία του Νέρωνος'. But it is still a very explicit use of historical irony, with the contrasts spelled out for the reader in the last two lines, as though Cavafy was more interested in the dramatic structure which such a technique can impart to a poem than in any 'message' which the incident might convey.

In his later historical poems Cavafy found much more subtle ways to present this sort of historical irony. 'Στα 200 Π.Χ.' is an excellent example. The poem starts with part of the phrase which, according to Plutarch, Alexander the Great caused to be inscribed upon the treasures which he sent back to Greece after his victorious campaigns in the East. It then switches to a first-person plural voice which could indicate a group, or a single person who identifies himself with his audience. The voice is not given an identity or context until 1.22, where we learn that it represents the Greeks of the East, the inheritors of the lands conquered by Alexander. The impression is of a speaker, himself an Alexandrian, Antiochean or something such, who, in the year 200 B.C., is reading Alexander's inscription and reflecting upon it. The poem then builds upon a series of historical ironies. In ll.2-11 the speaker explains the Spartans' refusal to take part in Alexander's expedition as the product of their pride, not to say arrogance. To the Spartans it was unthinkable for a Panhellenic military expedition not to be under Spartan command. They saw themselves as synonymous with Greek military power. The speaker seems to accept the legitimacy of this attitude in 1.12:

Είναι κι αυτή μια στάσις. Νοιώθεται.

Then, in ll.13-17, he destroys it by juxtaposing the absence of the Spartans with the size of Alexander's victories at the River Granicus (334 B.C.), at Issus (33 B.C.) and near Arbela (331 B.C.):

Έτοι, πλήν Λακεδαιμονίων στόν Γρανικό·
και στην Ισσό μετά· και στην τελειωτική
την μάχη, όπου εσαρώθη ο φοβερός στράτος
που στ' Άρβηλα συγκέντρωσαν οι Πέρσαι:
που απ' τ' Άρβηλα ξεκίνησε γιά νίκην, κ' εσαρώθη.

The military reality of Alexander's conquests shows that, in having such a high opinion of their own importance, the Spartans were living in the past. The speaker then reflects on the new great Greek world which stemmed from those victories, a world which made Sparta into a forgotten provincial backwater. Alexander's inscription neatly sums up the way in which a nation can be overtaken by events. The speaker expands on the vastness and variety of the new Greek world, and ends

14

by contemptuously dismissing the Spartans as now insignificant. The first level of irony is, then, the gap between the Spartans' view of themselves and the historical reality. The second level comes from the title. The year is 200 B.C. The Romans are about to start their gradual destruction and occupation of the Greek kingdoms which sprang up in the wake of Alexander: Philip V of Macedon will be defeated in 197 B.C., Antiochus the Great of Syria in 190 B.C. By 168 B.C. Macedon will become a Roman possession, and in 163 B.C., as we saw just now, the Romans will be in a position to interfere in the internal affairs of the Ptolemies in Egypt. The speaker's pride in the military conquests of Alexander and the Greek occupation of the East is as misplaced as was Sparta's pride before him.

There is however one further irony in the text, and it is by no means the least. The last of the Greek achievements listed by the speaker is the spread of the Greek language, the spoken κοινή, as far as the borders of India:

Και την Κοινήν Ελληνική Λαλιά
ως μέσα στην Βακτριανή την πήγαμεν, ως τους Ινδούς.

The irony here is that the coming Roman conquest will never eradicate this triumph of the Greek language. The poem itself, written in Greek, in Alexandria, two thousand years later, is testimony to the fact. What the speaker has placed at the climax of his list of sources of pride is indeed the one achievement which history will not reverse.

There might appear to be an unbridgeable gap between the relatively naive use of historical irony for dramatic effect in Cavafy's early poems and the elaborate layering of it in 'Στα 200 Π.Χ.'. But, in a sense, all these poems can be seen as exercises on the theme of the gap between illusion and reality. At first Cavafy treats the theme rather literally. Then he takes examples of historical events and uses more complex techniques, in which the personality of historical, or historically plausible, characters plays a greater part. Eventually he creates poems in which a

15

number of historical ironies can be deduced from different aspects of the poem: the title, the events discussed, the speaker's attitudes. So far we have looked at poems in which the gap between illusion and reality can be clearly measured. This is because, in each of the poems examined, an historical event or events undermines the validity of the world-view of the central character. But in many of Cavafy's later poems this is not the case. In these poems he sets two different world-views side by side. In this way he can explore the ironies which arise when two different sets of illusions confront one another. Such poems are inevitably much more ambiguous in their overall effect.

Take, for example, 'Ἡγεμών ἐκ Δυτικῆς Λιβύης'. The opening four lines of this poem are carefully arranged to discomfort the reader. First a simple statement:

Ἄρεσε γενικῶς στην Ἀλεξάνδρεια,

the subject of the verb being held over. Then the slightly deflatory revelation of how briefly he was in the city:

τες δέκα μέρες που διέμεινεν αυτού,

Next, in l.3, we find out who is being talked about:

ο ηγεμών εκ Δυτικῆς Λιβύης.

But l.4 offers us the prince's name: Aristomenes, son of Menelaos. Not only is this a quite disconcerting name for an African ruler, it is also a very disconcerting pair of names. Both Aristomenes and Menelaos were classical heroes. But whereas the latter was a king of Sparta, the former was a hero of the second Messenian war *against* Sparta.

So far the poem seems to present a factual portrait, yet the details of it ring slightly false. In ll.5-10 the factual portrait appears to continue, settling any doubts raised by the opening lines. A quiet, modest, intellectual figure emerges. Lines 11-12 offer a separate voice, the voice of public opinion speculating on this image:

θάταν βαθύς στες σκέψεις, διεδίδετο,
κ' οι τέτοιοι τ'όχουν να μη μιλούν πολλά.

All the details are positive. Then without warning, the second stanza rejects what we have been told in the first. It reveals the African as a fraud, a Greek only on the surface. The language is sarcastic: he is Ένας τυχαίος, αστείος άνθρωπος, scared of spoiling the goodish impression he has made. The suspicions aroused by the incongruities of ll. 1-4, then allayed, are now seen to have been justified. But the end of the stanza attacks the Alexandrians, too, for the fun they make of those who make mistakes in their Greek. And what an irony that the princeling has been able to impose so successfully on people who pride themselves on their sharpness! Are the clashing nuances of a name like 'Aristomenes, son of Menelaos' lost on the Alexandrians themselves?

The double point of the poem is now apparently made. What does the short final stanza add? Well, it adds the viewpoint of the central character, the frustration of a man crammed with things to say which he cannot, or dare not, express because he does not have command of the linguistic forms which society requires him to use. The poem, suddenly, is not just about social conformity, about passing oneself off as something one is not. It is also about the tyranny of linguistic conformity, and the way in which it can crush self-expression. For a Greek poet of the turn of the century, aware of the katharevousa-demotic controversy, and more especially for a poet of the Diaspora whose language has been criticised by both camps in the linguistic struggle, the idea of having to force oneself into an artificial linguistic form (whether katharevousa or the so-called pure demotic) was clearly a live issue. This poem seems to ridicule the prince for his cowardice and his pretensions, to criticise the Alexandrians for their intolerance and throw doubt on their judgement, and to express a certain sympathy for the effect that the linguistic predicament has upon its victim. These attitudes cannot all be attributed to the same voice.

In fact, if we look at the language of the poem itself, the sense of a number of competing points of view is very clear. The division between the first two stanzas is not merely typographical and thematic. It is also linguistic. The description in stanza one is scattered with formal touches—the verb forms διέμεινεν and διεδίδετο, the form υιός, all the adverbs in —ως, the enclitic δε in l.10. Only the words of the approving Alexandrians in ll. 11-12 are colloquial in vocabulary and construction:

> Θάταν βαθύς στές σκέψεις [...]
> κ' οι τέτοιοι τ'όχουν φυσικό να μη μιλούν πολλά.

The second stanza, on the other hand, is quite consciously colloquial in tone throughout—particularly in such details as τίποτε, επάνω κάτω, καλούτσικην, τον πάρουν στο ψιλό—and is devoid of formal touches. Because of this change of forms, the voice of this stanza seems to be quite different from that of the first ten lines. And the content separates it from the voice of ll. 11-12 quoted above. The third stanza then reverts, with its use of μη δέος and ουκ ολίγον. The linguistic link thus created between first and third stanzas, and the contrast with the second, adds another level to the ambiguities of the poem. The language forced onto the princeling is not that of the approving Alexandrians of the first stanza or of the critical voice in stanza two: but the poem itself can contain, and harmonise, all three.

There is no clear standard by which we can judge the competing attitudes in 'Ηγεμών εκ Δυτικής Λιβύης'. By ironising both the princeling and the Alexandrians, by offering both a critique of the victim and a degree of sympathy for him, Cavafy has brought out the relativity of all cultural judgments. In 'Ο Ιουλιανός και οι Αντιοχείς' he does the same with moral and religious judgments. It is possible to take the poem at its face value, and to read into it the words of an independent speaker recording with approval how the Antiocheans rejected the Emperor Julian's attacks on pleasure. This is in fact the standard way to read the poem, as Keeley does in *Cavafy's Alexandria* (p.121). Cavafy is supposed to be contrasting the puritanical authoritarianism of paganism, at least of Julian's kind, with the tolerance and flexibility of early Christianity, and to be approving the fact that Christianity is more sympathetic to the περιλάλητος βίος της Αντιοχείας [...] ο απόλυτα καλαίσθητος which (according to Keeley) Cavafy's poetry celebrates.

But there is another, a very different way in which the poem can be read. It is written in an apparently narrative tense, the imperfect, but the sense of speech is added by the use of exclamation (in the first and last stanzas), question (Να τ' αρνηθούν αυτά, για να προσέξουν κιόλας τί;), short, verbless sentences:

Τες περι των ψευδών θεών αερολογίες του,
τες ανιαρές περιαυτολογίες·
την παιδαριώδη του θεατροφοβία·
την άχαρι σεμνοτυφία του· τα γελοία του γένεια.

and the final elliptical colloquial exaggeration 'εκατό φορές'. Suppose we see in it, not the comments on an external speaker, but a piece of 'free indirect speech', an indirect representation of the thoughts of the Antiocheans themselves? The style then allows opinion to pass as fact, because it seems to be objectively reported (in the 3rd person) rather than subjectively expressed (1st person). Two views of life are being explored, those of Julian and those of the citizens of Antioch: but the views of the former are only recorded through the eyes of the latter. The epigraph from Julian's *Misopogon* simply reminds us of what the Antiocheans support against Julian. In the name of Christ and the late Christian emperor Constantius, Julian's former opponent, they support a life of self-indulgence and frivolity. The poem is thus built around an inherent irony.

For the poem to be taken this way, its structure has to be seen as a

C. P. Cavafy

determining factor in the way we react to the content, because it reveals
the order of priorities of the Antiocheans. The opening lines express
amazement at the idea of renouncing the beauty of life:

Ήτανε δυνατόν ποτέ ν' απαρνηθούν
την έμορφή τους διαβίωσι [...] !

This beauty is immediately redefined in terms of variety and amusement.
But the single concrete example given, the theatre, links art to sexuality—a covert way of referring to the pornographic theatrical displays
which the Eastern Empire had adopted from the Romans:

[...] το λαμπρό τους
θέατρον όπου μια ένωσις εγένονταν της Τέχνης
με τες ερωτικές της σάρκας τάσεις!

The justification for this immorality, which is conceded at the start of the
second stanza, is not so much that it is a compound of sensual and
aesthetic pleasure, as that it is a source of fame:

[...] 'Αλλ' είχαν την ικανοποίησι που ο βίος τους
ήταν ο περιλάλητος βίος της Αντιοχείας.

This is a society in which aestheticism and sensuality have declined into
indulgence and sensationalism.
    The following line is a pivot in the poem, introducing the attack on
Julian:

Τες περί των ψευδών θεών αερολογίες του,
τες ανιαρές περιαυτολογίες·
την παιδαριώδη του θεατροφοβία·
την άχαρι σεμνοτυφία του· τα γελοία του γένεια.

20

The order of the points made is again significant. The emperor's metaphysical speculation is dismissed first, then his boasting, hostility to the theatre and prudishness. His *beard* is kept for the climax of the list. The elements of the attack are in what would normally be seen as reverse order of importance. The adjectives reflect the same sort of frivolous value scale: boring (12), childish (13), graceless (14), ridiculous (14). What the Antiocheans hold against Julian are the trivial and superficial things. What they care most about is appearances. They condemn themselves, out of their own mouths, of frivolity, and they make themselves all the more absurd for doing so in the name of Christ and Constantius. They are of course right about Julian: history proves them so. But their rejection of him is for all the wrong reasons.

Now, I have given the above interpretation of 'Ο Ιουλιανός και οι Αντιοχείς' not because I wish to reject the traditional reading of the sort put forward by Keeley, but because it is at least as justifiable as the traditional reading. Neither interpretation can be definitive: neither can be ignored. The difference between the readings depends on who we think is speaking. Is it an external voice who we are directed to accept? Or is it an internal voice which is undermined by internal ironies? Side by side, the two readings show the relativity of the kinds of judgment made by both Julian and the Antiocheans. If we do not know who we are listening to, we find it difficult to assess the value of their words. Before we look further at the ironic possibilities which Cavafy extracts from this fact, perhaps we should look briefly at the question of voice and voices in his poetry in a more general sense.

5. The voices in Cavafy's poetry

Cavafy's poetry could in general be called *evaluative*. It is not primarily trying to convey pictures or emotions or physical sensations, but ways of looking at the world. The descriptive, emotive and sensual elements in it are filtered through a voice or voices, a speaking character, and our

21

C. P. Cavafy

response to those elements cannot be separated from our response to that character. I use the phrase 'speaking character' because the voice may, grammatically, be a simple 1st or 2nd person, or, as in some of the 'historical' poems, an independent character (e.g. 'Εύνοια του Αλεξάνδρου Βάλα') speaking in the first person. The voice may even, as we have seen, be the inner voice, the thoughts of a character, presented in 'free indirect speech'. The same element of a mind intellectually reflecting upon certain actions and emotions is present in many of the third person narratives, whether their settings are historical ('Εις Ιταλικήν παραλίαν') or contemporary ('Ήλθε για να διαβάσει').

Now, in some poems this sense of a mind at work, filtering experience and conveying a personal response to it, is given in an undeveloped form. In the 'philosophical' poems, which Cavafy wrote relatively early on in his poetic career, there is often a second person grammatical voice which represents someone—'the poet', let us say— explaining life to someone else. Neither the speaker nor the addressee is given an identity or a personality. Indeed, the person addressed could be a projection of the speaker's own self. 'Η πόλις', 'Η σατραπεία', 'Μάρτιαι Ειδοί', 'Απολείπειν ο θεός Αντώνιον', and 'Ο Θεόδοτος' are examples of this. In practice this has the effect of conferring upon the speaker the status of sage, dispensing a wisdom which is made both more striking and more weighty by the classical parallels in which it is wrapped. From these poems with a neutral 'speaking character', who simply adopts the role of sage, we can move to another group of poems, usually short and in either 1st or 2nd person voice, such as 'Θυμήσου, σώμα', 'Επέστρεφε' and 'Για ν'άρθουν', which define the speaker in more detail in terms of his views on memory, time, art. Here we have the speaker as aesthete, or as creative artist, as well as sage. Slightly more complex still are those poems, often erotic, containing a first person grammatical voice, again identifiable with 'the poet'—e.g. 'Θάλασσα του πρωιού', 'Το διπλανό τραπέζι', 'Εν εσπέρα', 'Ο ήλιος του απογεύματος'—in which an attitude to the world is being sketched which creates a sense of the speaker as a *character*. Let us pause and see

22

how this is achieved in 'Σ' ἕνα βιβλίο παληό'. The theme of the poem is simple. The speaker has come across a water-colour sketch of a handsome young man in an old book, and draws certain conclusions about the boy's character. A subject of this sort has a descriptive potential which is not in fact exploited in the poem. Indeed, the balance of detail in some parts is superficially rather oddly chosen. Having been told that the book is old, we are given the additional gloss that it is about a hundred years old and that the artist is very skilful— details which add little to our sense of the picture itself. Yet about the young man who is its subject we learn nothing detailed beyond the fact that he has vivid brown eyes. The key phrases, ιδεώδη χείλη and ιδεώδη μέλη, do not contribute to a physical picture (except in so far as the word 'ideal' applied to the male body has wider associations for any reader already familiar with Cavafy's poetry). The reference to limbs suggests that the young man is shown full-length, and the phrase

(εὔκολα νοιώθονταν η ιδέα του καλλιτέχνου)

suggests that the eroticism which the speaker finds in the manner of portrayal is implicit rather than part of the subject of the painting. The balance of the poem is not directed to recreating the painting at all. It concerns itself with evoking the response of the *speaker* to the painting. Phrases such as εκλεκτή εμορφιά, ιδεώδη χείλη, ιδεώδη μέλη reflect the standards and preoccupations of the speaker, while the 'moral' phrases—για όσους αγαπούνε κάπως υγιεινά, μες στ' οπωσδήποτε επιτετραμμένον μένοντες, που αναίσχυντα τ' αποκαλεί η τρεχάμενη ηθική—are ironic rejections of the sort of attitudes and language which are revealed, in the last phrase, to be those of the uninitiated.

The effect of the poem depends on the gradual penetration of the speaker's mind which we are offered. Gradually the poem changes from a formal, rather academic opening, with its almost pedantic references to περίπου εκατό ετών and καλλιτέχνου λίαν δυνατού, to the first

23

hints of sexual excitement in the isolated line in which an alternative, more suggestive title for the water-colour is offered:

> Πλην μάλλον ήρμοζε, << —του έρωτος των άκρως αισθητών >>.

Briefly the speaker's true feelings are masked behind the apparent acceptance of conventional moral vocabulary in ll.9-10:

> [...] για όσους αγαπούνε κάπως υγιεινά,
> μες στ' οπωσδήποτε επιτετραμμένον μένοντες,
> δεν ήταν προωρισμένος ο έφηβος

but he is unmasked eventually by the sensual response evident in εκλεκτή εμορφιά and developed in the phrases που φέρνουνε / την ηδονή εις αγαπημένο σώμα and τα ιδεώδη μέλη του πλασμένα για κρεββάτια. The revelation in the final line that the moral vocabulary so far used has been ironic is scarcely necessary. The poem translates into mental images a definitely physical response to the painting. The young man is a symbol of homosexual desirability, rather than an independent aesthetic presence. The poet is not trying to communicate the quality of the picture but the quality of its effect. What counts is the speaker's initial circumspectness, his reluctance to commit himself to a full confession and his growing excitement.

Stylistically it is only a short step from a poem of this sort to the creation of an independent first person speaker of the sort we find in 'Στα 200 Π.Χ.' and 'Εν μεγάλη Ελληνική αποικία, 200 Π.Χ.'. The poet merely has to use a context, usually a temporal one, which indicates that the speaking voice cannot be his own. But the relationship between the reader and the text is considerably changed by this projection of all the feelings and perceptions described in the poem onto a clearly independent character. And the relationship is changed again if the independent character is made part of a 3rd person narrative. It is very difficult (though not impossible) to create a sense of irony in a poem in which there is no clear distinction between the 'speaking character' and the poet himself, because irony depends on the existence of a perceptible contradiction between different views of the world, e.g. between the speaker and 'reality'. Hence, what form of voice Cavafy uses in a poem will have a considerable effect on what type and degree of irony he can build into it. To examine this further, let us look at two relatively complex poems on historical themes: 'Από την σχολήν του περιωνύμου φιλοσόφου' and ''Ας φρόντιζαν'.

'Από την σχολήν του περιωνύμου φιλοσόφου' starts with a typical piece of Cavafean impersonal narration. It tells the story of a young man who gets bored with a series of activities and decides to devote himself to pleasure (implicitly to homosexual debauchery) until his beauty fades. Not only is the voice addressing us at the outset of the poem anonymous, but so is the person who is being described: we do not know who the subject of έμεινε and βαρέθηκε is, and that subject remains nameless throughout the poem. We know merely, from the reference to Sakkas, that we are in Alexandria in the third century A.D. The apparently factual 3rd person narration continues until the second half of 1.4, where there is a shift into free indirect speech—the view of the Eparch as a fool is the personal judgment of the anonymous central character. This sense of mental speech (i.e. of a character's thought-processes) is confirmed by the syntax of 1.6:

τρισβάρβαρα τα ελληνικά των, οι άθλιοι.

This shift from narration to indirect speech sets the pattern for the rest of the poem. In stanza three the first three and a half lines are narrative, but the second three and a half lines are clearly the young man's thought, the tone of speech being marked by the exclamation πράγμα φρικτόν. In the fourth stanza the pattern is reversed: an inner reflection is followed by the description of the action. The fifth stanza is entirely narration, but the sixth and seventh are entirely in indirect speech.

25

C. P. Cavafy

So the poem has two basic voices, both in the third person: narrative and character. The character's voice is a consistent one. It is the voice of a slightly superior, disenchanted youth, who cares about style—he protests at the barbarity of the Greek spoken in political circles—and who puts high living above high principles—he decides not to become a Christian because he does not want his pagan parents to cut off his monthly allowance. The sense of superiority is conveyed by the way in which he calls the Eparch μωρός, his officials ξόανα and άθλιοι, and by his contemptuous reference to the great Sakkas as ο γέρος. The sense of disenchantment reaches its height in the final words, where he ridicules such concepts as family traditions and patriotism as merely high-sounding words:

Η τέλος, δυνατόν και στα πολιτικά
να επέστρεφεν–αξιεπαίνως ενθυμούμενος
τες οικογενειακές του παραδόσεις,
το χρέος προς την πατρίδα, κι άλλα ηχηρά παρόμοια.

The character's voice is therefore distinct in its values.

The narrative voice is more elusive. Initially it appears to be factual, neutral: it tells us how long the boy stayed with Sakkas, why he left, what he did next. But in stanza 4 it becomes full of highly charged language, as it informs us that the boy frequented dubious establishments in Alexandria:

[...] Έγινε ο θαμών
των διεφθαρμένων οίκων της Αλεξανδρείας

Note in particular the emphasis given by the musical patterning of l.16:

κάθε κρυφού καταγωγίου κραιπάλης.

This apparently moralising tone is, however, subverted by the following stanza, which attributes to divine gift the fact that the boy's beauty fitted

26

him for a life of debauchery. And at this point the narrative voice withdraws altogether. What can the reader make of this portrait? There is a cynical, somewhat precious world-weariness about the central character which gives us grounds to doubt his evidently high view of himself. But the narrative voice stubbornly declines to criticise him. It leaves us to accept his criticism of Alexandrian life and institutions as valid. And after appearing to disapprove of his immorality, it withdraws that disapproval and abandons us to his world-view. Only the title creates an element of incontrovertible irony. This disabused youth, concerned only with pleasure and with projecting the right image, is a product of the philosophical school of the greatest philosopher of his age: Ammonios Sakkas was a neo-Platonic philosopher of the third century A.D. and the teacher of three more famous Greek thinkers, Origen, Longinus and Plotinus. But this irony is left undeveloped. Does the fault for what happens lie with the philosophy or the boy? The voices of the poem decline to tell us. They create a character; that is all. This is, perhaps, the ultimate form of irony: the irony of relativity. As in 'Ο Ιουλιανός και οι Αντιοχείς', though by a different method, the reader is left to feel that all value judgments are relative to the person making them, as much as to the thing judged.

Compare 'Από την σχολήν του περιωνύμου φιλοσόφου' with ''Ας φρόντιζαν', and you will see how a difference of voice changes the reader's perspective. In this latter poem we have an exclusively 1st person voice, another anonymous young cynic, an Antiochean, though of an earlier period (the historical figures referred to place the time of the poem between 128 and 123 B.C.). In his monologue he reviews himself and his prospects. In so doing he reveals his value system and thereby unconsciously offers a self-critique. It is for the reader to deduce the ironic gap between his interpretation of himself and the reality which it betrays.

The first stanza introduces the young man to us as almost homeless and penniless. From the emphasis on Antioch as αυτή η μοιραία πόλις and the reference to its expensive life we deduce two things. That the speaker is a bit of a playboy, and that he refuses to take responsibility for what happens to himself. If he is broke, it is because

[...] η Αντιόχεια
όλα τα χρήματά μου τ'άφαγε

not because *he* has wasted it on riotous living.

The second stanza sets out his advantages: youth, health, an excellent command of Greek. Notice the comic clash between the evidence he adduces to prove his knowledge of Greek—he has read all the best classical authors—and the slangy way in which he expresses the idea:

(ξέρω και παραξέρω Αριστοτέλη, Πλάτωνα·
τί ρήτορας, τί ποιητάς, τί ό,τι κι αν πεις).

As his analysis goes on, he begins to give the impression of a man who will lay claim to competence in any area you care to name (the army, the civil service), to know all the right people (he is on good terms with some of the mercenary leaders), to have been in all the right places (he spent six months in Alexandria). All his claims have a tiny restriction built into them:

(1.9)   Από στρατιωτικά έχω μιάν ιδέα
(1.11)   Είμαι μπασμένος κάμποσο και στα διοικητικά
(1.13)   κάπως γνωρίζω [...] τα εκεί.

Not even he would go so far as to define himself as properly qualified in anything. But on the strength of this smattering of skills, he considers himself fully equipped for one task—to serve his country. Lines 15-19 are uncomfortably reminiscent of the high-sounding language about which the central character in 'Από την σχολήν του περιωνύμου φιλοσόφου' is so contemptuous:

'Όθεν φρονώ πώς είμαι στα γεμάτα
ενδεδειγμέγος γιά να υπηρετήσω αυτήν την χώρα,
την προσφιλή πατρίδα μου Συρία.

Σ' ο,τι δουλειά με βάλλουν θα πασχίσω
να είμαι στην χώρα οφέλιμος. Αυτή ειν' η πρόθεσίς μου.

Here, the language carries no hint of conscious irony on the part of the speaker. The irony comes, first, from the gap between the qualifications of the aspirant and the position aspired to, and second, between the expression of patriotism and the qualification of it which follows.

The basis of our hero's attitude is 'Whatever goes wrong won't be my fault', a stance for which we have been prepared by his explanation of his poverty in the first stanza. If he does not prosper in the service of Syria, it will be because his employers are idiots. Lines 29-31 finally strip bare his pretensions to patriotism—he acknowledges that none of those whose service he might seek are capable of doing Syria any good in any case:

Κ' είν' η συνείδησις μου ήσυχη
γιά το αψήφιστο της εκλογής.
Βλάπτουν κ' οι τρείς τους την Συρία το ίδιο.

Patriotism is an empty cause if there is no way of serving it. Maybe the three candidates *are* equally unappetising but that is not a justification for his willingness to serve under any of them. Characteristically the final stanza throws the responsibility for the situation onto fate. We have all met the type: the moaner, who is always putting the blame for his troubles in life on an anonymous 'them'—if only 'they' would do something about the world around him, everything would be fine. Here, the speaker excuses himself as Ζητώ [...] να μπαλοθώ, only trying to scrape by. The desire to be useful to his country merely covers a desire to do the best for himself that he can.

In ''Aς φρόντιζαν', Cavafy uses a 1st person voice to create a character who unmasks himself, and in so doing unmasks the barren political climate in which he lives. The character revealed has distinct similarities with that it 'Από την σχολήν του περιωνύμου φιλοσόφου'. Both are willing to try anything and committed to nothing, both find everyone else a fool, both attribute everything to the hand of fate or to a god. But unlike in the latter poem, where narrative voice and the character's voice create a curiously neutral picture, the reader of the former poem is left in little doubt as to the values, or lack of them, of the world of the poem. This is because, though the world view to which both poems contribute is in many ways similar, the poetic process by which that world is conveyed in entirely different.

Identification of the forms and techniques of Cavafean irony goes some way to explaining the 'tone of voice' which W.H. Auden found it so hard to pin down. It also fits in with the feeling that Cavafy is not studying themes or issues, not constructing a mythical Alexandria or trying to build up a continuous picture of a section of history, but producing a series of artistic variations on the problem of the instability of human values and judgments. What we have so far not examined is what are the distinctively *poetic* qualities of this exploration of ephemerality and flux.

PART II: POETIC TECHNIQUE

Many people think of the poetry of Cavafy as, paradoxically, unpoetic, because it lacks the elaborate vocabulary and the complex imagery of poets such as Palamas and Elytis. Such people overlook the fact that Cavafy uses a large range of other, perhaps less obvious, poetic techniques. In particular, he pays great attention to the rhythm and sound of what he writes. He chooses and places his individual words and grammatical structures for specific effects. He is in fact a master of many sorts of patterning. Perhaps the proof of his mastery is precisely that his techniques are so rarely obtrusive that they can easily be overlooked.

A complete catalogue of Cavafy's techniques would be impossible to compile, extremely boring, and probably not very helpful, since each takes its meaning from the individual context in which it is used. I shall look briefly at various classes of technical effect for which we should be alert when analysing a Cavafy poem. Then I shall examine a series of poems, looking at the ways in which the individual elements combine to create an overall effect.

1. Rhythm
There are three main elements which shape the rhythm in a Cavafy poem: the stanza shape, the metre, and *caesura* (breaking a metrical unit where one grammatical unit ends and another begins) and *enjambement* (breaking a grammatical unit across the end of one line and the beginning of the next). Critics are divided on the precise nature of Cavafean

31

metrics, though most agree that he uses a basically iambic line, and uses it in an unexpectedly fluid, rather English way, perhaps influenced by his reading of nineteenth-century English poets. To a certain extent the detailed analysis of the metre does not matter as long as the ear catches the relationship between the number of syllables in a line and the placing of the main stresses. Another important factor is whether the line ends on a stressed syllable (a 'masculine' ending) or a single unstressed one (a 'feminine' ending). As an example, look at 'Δέησις':

13 syllables	I tha̱l I assa I sta va̱th I i tis I pi̱r' en I an na̱f I ti
13 syllables	I ma̱n I a tou I ani̱ I xeri I pye̱n I i ky ana̱f I ti
13 syllables	stim pa I nayi̱ I a brosta̱ I en(a) i I psilo̱ I keri̱
14 syllables	ya n(a) e I pistre̱p I si gri̱ I gora I ke nan I kali̱ I keri̱
12 syllables	ke ol I o pros I ton a̱n I emo I sti̱ni I t'avti̱
14 syllables	Alla I eno I prose̱f I hete I ke de̱ I ete I avti̱
13 syllables	i (i)ko̱n I akou̱ I i sov I ari̱ ke li I pime̱n I i
15 syllables	xe̱vron I das pos I den th'al I thi pya̱ I o yio̱s I pou pe I rime̱n I i

Certain rhythmic differences are immediately obvious. The first and last couplet are linked by the trailing effect of their 'feminine' endings. The third couplet differs sharply from the others in that both its lines have only three significant stresses. The last line is the only one to have five stresses. The rhythmic variations create patterns. The three 'characters' of the poem, the sea, the mother and the ikon, all appear in 13 syllable lines. The purpose of the prayer (l.4) and the act of praying (l.6) are both expressed in 14 syllable lines. In the first couplet, the sea and its actions are described with exactly the same stress pattern as the mother and hers. But the difference between the lines is emphasised too, in that the sea's action is grammatically complete, whereas the mother's requires an enjambement into line 3. The only strong rhythmic break within a foot (1.7), the caesura ακούει, σοβαρή emphasises the moment of dramatic irony—however attentively the ikon listens, there is nothing it can do to undo the action of the sea. This 'dramatic' use of metre to emphasise relationships and high points in the text is characteristic of many Cavafy poems.

Stanza shape in Cavafy is a more problematic topic. There are a handful of poems in couplets ('Δέησις', 'Τείχη', 'Του μαγαζιού', 'Η μάχη της Μαγνησίας', 'Ο Ιουλιανός εν Νικομηδεία', 'Το 31 Π.Χ. στήν Αλεξάνδρεια') and a smaller number still in other regular patterns such as quatrains ('Μονοτονία', 'Che fece ... il gran rifiuto', 'Αιμιλιανός Μονάη', 'Ιασή Τάφος') and terza rima ('Ενας γέρος'). Occasional poems have a special structure of their own, e.g. 'Ούτος Εκείνος', whose palindromic rhyme-scheme* A B C D C C D C B A is arranged into a quatrain flanked by two three-line stanzas. Most of the poems, however, are divided into stanzas of unequal length, or in the case of short poems are sometimes in a single verse paragraph. But whether regular or irregular, the divisions into stanzas are not arbitrary in Cavafy. They mark stages in the development of the theme and mood.

A simple example is 'Του πλοίου':

Τον μοιάζει βέβαια η μικρή αυτή,
με το μολύβι απεικόνισίς του.

Γρήγορα καμωμένη, στο κατάστρωμα του πλοίου·
ένα μαγευτικό απόγευμα.
Το Ιόνιον πέλαγος ολόγυρα μας.

Τον μοιάζει. Όμως τον θυμούμαι σαν πιό έμορφο.
Μέχρι παθήσεως ήταν αισθητικός,
κι αυτό εφώτιζε την εκφρασί του.

---

* I.e. the second half of the rhyme scheme is the mirror image of the first.

C. P. Cavafy

Πιό έμορφος με φανερώνεται
τώρα πού η ψυχή μου τον ανακαλεί, απ' τον Καιρό.

Απ' τον Καιρό. Είν' όλ' αυτά τα πράγματα πολύ παληά—
το σκίτσο, και το πλοίο, και το απόγευμα.

Here the first stanza (ll.1-2) introduces the pencil sketch and the idea of likeness. In the second stanza (ll.3-5) Cavafy evokes the moment at which the sketch was done. The third (ll.6-10) reflects on the beauty of the subject of the sketch and superior power of memory to preserve that beauty from the power of time. The final stanza (ll.11-12) links aspects of the subject matter of the first three—the sketch, where it was done, and the irrevocable passage of time. The theme of the power of memory generates the longest of the stanzas, but the fact that the final stanza has the same two-line form as the first, and the absence from it of any mention of the beautiful young man, emphasises the transitory nature of the recall. On this occasion, in the uneasy struggle between time, memory and art, ultimately time seems to have won. So the function of the varying stanza shape has been to 'punctuate' the stages of the drama which the poem acts out.

Before we leave the subject of metre and verse form, we should perhaps give special attention to the poems in what seems to be an experimental form peculiar to Cavafy. These are the poems in which each line is physically divided into two on the page. There are no less than seventeen of them, plus one in which two-thirds of the lines are divided. This last, 'Ομνύει', is a straightforward case. The split lines, 1-4, contain the determination to reform and the temptation of the night. As that temptation is repeated in line 4, the metre, like the subject, gives way and '... returns/ forlorn to the same fatal joy' (στην ίδια μοιραία χαρά, χαμένος, ξαναπιαίνει). The metre is thus an ironic mirror to the subject matter, ironic because the attempt to become conventional is couched in unconventional metre, and the relapse into unconventionality is accompanied by the fall back into metrical convention. 'Ομνύει'

34

seems to have been the first poem in which Cavafy attempted this sort of metrical pattern. In the later poems he was to explore the extra possibilities of rhyme, assonance*, enjambement and masculine/feminine rhythmic patters which the half-lines offer. In 'Εἰς Ἰταλικήν παραλίαν' for example it is possible to read the left-hand column of ll.1-6 as a self-contained grammatical unit:

Ο Κῆμος Μενεδώρου,
τον βίον του περνά
ως συνειθιζουν τούτοι
μές στά πολλά τα πλούτη

Μα σήμερα είναι λίαν,
σύννους και κατηφής.

This is, in a sense, the whole of the setting of the poem, and it has its own internal structure. The characterisation of Kimos as a wealthy playboy is rounded off by an internal rhyme (τούτοι/πλούτη), emphasising that the contrast in mood in 5-6 is a new phase in the poem. Only at the dramatic highpoint, in lines 7-9, does the 'separate' continuity of grammar and sense in the left-hand column break down:

	Κοντά στήν παραλίαν,
με άκραν μελαγχολίαν	βλέπει πού εκφορτώνουν
τα πλοία με την λείαν	εκ της Πελοποννήσου.
Λάφυρα ελληνικά	η λεία της Κορίνθου.

But here another pattern takes over. Already in 5-6 there is a rhyme between λίαν at the end of 5a and παραλίαν at the end of 6b. This rhyme

---

* Assonance is the matching of stressed vowels in two words, but not of the following consonants, e.g. μέρα, μέγα.

extends to μελαγχολίαν (7a) and λείαν (8a). Similarly (10b) θεμιτόν rhymes with (11a) δυνατόν. And the last words of the poem, καμιάν επιθυμίαν, form a final musical link with the —λίαν rhymes of the previous stanza. The left-hand column of 1-6 does indeed introduce the setting and the chief character. But the details we need if we are to understand what happens are all in the right-hand column: the tension between being an inhabitant of Italy and a part of the Greek diaspora. The rhymes of the second stanza then link the key words of place, cause and effect: the shore, the plunder, the melancholy. The boy is saddened by the sight of the plunder brought back by the Roman consul L. Mummius in 146 B.C. after the destruction of Corinth, because the booty represents the destruction of his cultural and historical roots. The rhyme θεμιτόν /δυνατόν emphasises the parallelism of the two concepts: for the moment he neither should nor could give himself up to the carefree, pleasure-loving existence which is his normal life-style. And the final echo of the —λίαν rhyme in καμιάν επιθυμίαν reiterates this change of mood. The split-line verse form has allowed Cavafy to exploit a large range of grammatical and musical oppositions and links in order to strengthen the thematic patterns of the poem. No two of the poems of this kind use the possibilities of the form in the same way, and all of them repay close study.

2. Sound patterning
In Cavafy's poetry sound patterning plays a great part in shaping the poems. It occurs in two forms: rhyme (including assonance and internal rhyme) and patterns of recurring vowels and consonants within the line.

2.2 rhyme
More than fifty of Cavafy's poems are entirely or largely in rhyme.

Sometimes the rhyme schemes are simple. Ὁ Ἰουλιανός εν Νικομηδεία', for example, is in rhyming couplets (AA, BB etc). 'Τείχη' is rhymed AB, AB CD, CD. More elaborate but equally regular structures exist: 'Σοφοί δε προσιόντων' (see below) is rhymed ABCAD EDCEB. In all these poems the musical pattern is immediately obvious to the ear. But what is it for? A major function of Cavafean rhyme is to bring together different words which have a special relationship in a poem. Take a simple example. 'Η ψυχές των γερόντων'. The rhyme scheme is ABBCCBBA. It could hardly be more regular. Most of the rhymes are grammatical, i.e. they rhyme the same part of speech in the same case, number and gender. The A rhymes are adjectives describing the decrepit nature of the old men's bodies: the B rhymes are the noun ψυχές and a series of equally derogatory adjectives describing the souls. The C rhyme, on the other hand, juxtaposes two verbs which are the focus of contradictory sentiments:

και πώς βαρυούνται την ζωή την άθλια που τραβούνε.

Πώς τρέμουν μην την χάσουνε και πώς την αγαπούνε

emphasising the irony of the way in which men cling to their lives even when they cease to have any value.

The effect is more important if the words brought together by the rhyme are physically further apart in the poem. Take 'Σοφοί δε προσιόντων', for example.

Θεοί μεν γαρ μελλόντων, άνθρωποι δε γιγνο-
μένων, σοφοί δε προσιόντων αισθάνονται.
Φιλόστρατος, Τα ες τον Τυανέα
Απολλώνιον, VIII, 7.

Οι άνθρωποι γνωρίζουν τα γινόμενα.
Τα μέλλοντα γνωρίζουν οι θεοί,

πλήρεις και μόνοι κάτοχοι πάντων των φώτων.
Εκ των μελλόντων οι σοφοί τα προσερχόμενα
αντιλαμβάνονται. Η ακοή
αυτών κάποτε εν ώραις σοβαρών σπουδών
ταράττεται. Η μυστική βοή
τους έρχεται των πλησιαζόντων γεγονότων.
Και την προσέχουν ευλαβείς. Ενώ εις την οδόν
έξω, ουδέν ακούουν οι λαοί.

Here only the C rhymes have no special function. The A rhymes are the
present and the future (τα γινόμενα and τα προσερχόμενα), the D
rhymes link the hearing of the wise men (ακοή) and the special 'clamour
of approaching events' (βοή) which penetrates it, the E rhyme (σπουδών,
οδών) contrasts the environment of the wise and that of the common man,
and the B rhymes oppose the all-seeing gods and the all-ignorant people
(θεοί and λαοί). In other words, the oppositions between different types
of perception which the poem explores, and which are developed by
other types of patterns within the poem (e.g. the chiastic arrangement of
lines 1-2: noun verb object/object verb noun), are underlined by the
juxtapositions of words created in the rhyme scheme.

This sort of 'relationship by rhyme' is strengthened if the rhyme
itself is a strong one. The more elements in a pair of words there are in
common, the stronger—or 'richer' the rhyme. In the poem we have just
been looking at, θεοί/λαοί is a weak rhyme, because only the last
syllable rhymes. (Cavafy has chosen to make the only weak rhyme in the
poem the rhyme which links the two words, men and gods, which have
the least link in reality.) In the same poem σπουδών/οδών is a stronger
rhyme because it has two common elements: φώτων/γεγονότων which
has four sounds in common, and γινόμενα/προερχόμενα, which has
five, are really rich rhymes. Indeed, Cavafy has an eye for the effects to
be got from rhyming words which sound identical. An obvious example,
is the rhyming of the two τείχη/τύχη—walls and fate—in 'Walls',
where the walls *are* the fate of the person shut in by them. A more

elaborate example still is the rhyming of θα μένει (will remain) and θαμένη (buried) in 'Η πόλις', emphasising that change through movement is impossible.

What I have said so far about the effect of conventional end-of-line rhyme applies also to internal rhyme, particularly in the group of poems in which the poem falls visually into two groups on the page (e.g. 'Εν τω μήνι Αθύρ', 'Για ν'άρθουν', 'Εκόμισα εις την Τέχνη', 'Τεχνουργός κρατήρων'). In 'Εις Ιταλικήν παραλίαν', as we saw, the rhyme —ian links lines 5a, 6b, 7a, 8a and 12b, a fact all the more noticeable since the poem does not otherwise rhyme. The words and phrases brought together by this means are λίαν, παραλίαν, μελαγχολίαν, λείαν and καμιάν επιθυμίαν. In other words, the rhyming links the place (the shore), the mood of the protagonist (extreme gloom) and the cause (the sight of the treasures looted from Corinth which are being unloaded on the shore). The essentials of the poem are musically emphasised by this discreet device.

Creating relationships between words is by no means the only function of rhyme in Cavafy's poetry. Another important function of his rhymes can be to highlight a thematic structure within a poem. An obvious example can be found in 'Αιμιλιανός Μονάη, Αλεξανδρεύς, 628-655 M.X.'. The first two stanzas, the poem supposedly written by the character in the title, rhyme richly ABAB CDCD. The third stanza has two unrhymed lines framing a weak rhyme, EFFG, the effect being to isolate the character's name and the final fact of his death. A much more complex example of structuring through rhyme can be found in 'Ζωγραφισμένα':

Την εργασία μου την προσέχω και την αγαπώ.
Μα της συνθέσεως μ' αποθαρρύνει σήμερα η βραδύτης.
Η μέρα μ' επηρέασε. Η μορφή της
όλο και σκοτεινιάζει. 'Ολο φυσά και βρέχει.
Πιότερο επιθυμώ να δω παρά να πω.
Στην ζωγραφιάν αυτή κυττάζω τώρα

39

ένα ωραίο αγόρι πού σιμά στη βρύση
επλάγιασεν, αφού θ' απέκαμε 'α τρέχει.
Τι ωραίο παιδι· τι θείο μεσημέρι το έχει
παρμένο πιά γιά να το αποκοιμίσει. —
Κάθομαι και κυττάζω έτσι πολλήν ώρα.
Και μες στην τέχνη πάλι, ξεκουράζομαι απ' την
δούλεψή της.

Here, the rhyme scheme ABBCADECCEDB appears random. But if we
look at the 'content', it is clear why the rhymes are distributed as they are.
Lines 1-5 and 12 are the framework, describing the mood of the speaker
before and after he looks at a painting. Lines 6 and 11 contain the act of
looking; 7-10 reproduce the picture of the beautiful boy lying beside the
fountain. So the rhyme DECCED picks out for us the thematic centre of
the poem, the 'art object', and the act of looking at it, in which the speaker
finds temporary refuge from the difficulties of his own art. And by
making the final line, expressing the aesthetic satisfaction of seeing
something beautiful, rhyme with lines 2 and 3, in which he describes the
problems of creating something beautiful, Cavafy sets up a deliberate
parallel between artist and spectator. For him, both of them are active
participants in the creative process.

In the above examples Cavafy uses the musical shape of a particular
rhyme pattern to emphasise a thematic structure. Another way of
creating a formal pattern of this sort is to harness technical oppositions
between types of rhyme. When discussing 'Η ψυχές των γερόντων'
above, I mentioned that nearly all the rhymes in the poem were 'grammatical'. The difference between grammatical and non-grammatical
rhymes can be used in just this way. Thus in 'Του μαγαζιού', the first
four rhyming couplets are rich non-grammatical rhymes, and these
describe the real works of art, the flowers which the jeweller has carved
in precious stone. The last couplet has a rhyme equally rich but much less
striking because grammatical: this couplet represents the jewellery—
fine of its kind—which the jeweller actually sells. Art and trade are thus

neatly separated by the rhymes.

So far I have discussed the ways in which the presence of rhyme helps to create meaning. But this brings about another possibility: the effect of the 'failure' of rhyme. One of the qualities of rhyme is to breed expectation. One word comes—where is the word to rhyme with it? The possibilities of subverting our expectation of rhyme for humorous effect are neatly explored by Cavafy in 'Εν μεγάλη Ελληνική αποικία, 200 Π.Χ.'. This is a quietly ironical poem in deliberately very prosaic language. The speaker, a citizen of an unspecified Greek colony just before Rome destroyed Greek political hegemony in the East, reflects dubiously on the the unsatisfactory state of the colony, but, after pondering on the prospect of political reform, manages to argue himself full-circle into feeling that perhaps the status-quo is best after all. Both rhyme and our expectations about rhyme play a major part in creating character in the poem, by building up a sense of someone whose enthusiasm for novelty is tempered by his desire to keep everything neatly fitted into the existing system.

First, look at the way that the first two stanzas are constructed. The rhyme scheme of lines 1-13 is AA, BB, C/AA, DD, C, EE, F/. So the single sentence which forms the first stanza starts with two rhyming couplets: Αποικία/αμφιβολία, εμπρός/καιρός. Now, the rhyming couplet is a very 'finished' form to the ear. But neither of these couplets finishes the sentence. Instead the stanza ends on a new sound, the 'ti' of Αναμορφωτή. In other words, the Political Reformer, who is to be the new broom in the colony, is a new broom in the rhyme scheme too.

The second stanza apparently offers us no rhyme for Αναμορφωτή. Instead it sets off on another single sentence which runs beyond a rhyming couplet, this time breaking in the middle of the second couplet. The speaker's enthusiasm for Political Reformers is already on the wane—Αναμορφωταί is rhymed with ποτέ. But the tenth line quite unexpectedly offers a belated rhyme for the fifth—a rhyme for Αν-αμορφωτή. But what a rhyme! κάθε τί, the most trivial rhyme you could think of, and on an enjambement too.

The speaker's doubts run on through yet another rhyming couplet, and into yet another new sound at the end of the stanza—αναβολῆς. This time the speaker seems to have decisively launched himself into a new phase of rhyme, along with his new topic, the reformers' unfortunate taste for sacrifices. The end-words of the first two lines of the third stanza introduce entirely new rhymes, GH. But lo and behold! the indecision of the speaker yet again presents us with a belated rhyme, ἐπισφαλής for αναβολῆς at the end of the previous stanza.

Lines 15-22, which parody the language of the reformers, and their endless negative instructions, are heavily repetitive musically: HFGIIIHH, with the same vowel in both the H and I rhymes, and finishing up on a triumphantly jingling couplet. The speaker seems to have got over his propensity for rhyme after-thoughts. Not a bit of it! Stanza 4, JJF, ends on a 'rhyme' (or perhaps an assonance, since F is really a rhyme in —lis) too long past for the ear to pick it up. And suddenly we are back at the beginning of the poem again: ABAKI/ BALALB, as the speaker stands all his original points on their head, leaving us, as with the rhyme, where we started, only not so. There is a particularly nice irony in the fact that rhyme is a weapon turned against both speaker and reformers.

2.2 Other forms of sound patterning

Nobody, of course, hears the rhymes in the artificial analytical way in which I have just presented them. They simply bring out a tendency which is inherent in the words actually spoken by the central character of the poem. The same is true of all the other forms of sound patterning which Cavafy uses. Far from being an unmusical poet, as many of his contemporaries asserted, he has an acute ear for the relationships which sound can create. Sometimes, of course, he plays with sound for harmony's sake, where harmony or beauty is part of his theme. E.g. 'Τεχνουργός κρατήρων' (lines 5-7):

κ' έθεσα εν τω μέσω   έναν ωραίον νέον,
γυμνόν, ερωτικόν·   μες στο νερό την κνήμη
την μιά του έχει ακόμη. —   Ικέτευσα, ω μνήμη, ...

Here the words o<u>reon</u>, <u>neon</u>, e<u>rotikon</u> and <u>nero</u> make one musical group, yim<u>n</u>on, <u>knimi</u>, a<u>komi</u>, i<u>k</u>etefsa and <u>mnimi</u> another, the 'n' linking the two groups. At the same time the vowels in the first line make a pattern of e, a, o, those in the second a pattern of e, i, o. The overall effect is gently melodious. Elsewhere this sort of patterning has a more specific function. In 'Μελαγχολία του Ιάσωνος Κλεάνδρου', the key words of the first three lines are all linked by sound pattern:

Το γήρασμα του σώματος και της μορφής μου
είναι πληγή από φρικτό μαχαίρι.
Δεν έχω εγκαρτέρησι καμιά.

(yi) γήρασμα / πληγή
(ma) γήρασμα / σώματος / μαχαίρι + (m) μορφής μου and καμιά
(eri) μαχαίρι / εγκαρτέρησι + (r) γήρασμα, μορφής, φρικτό
(t) σώματος / φρικτό / εγκαρτέρησι + το, του, της
(f) μορφής / φρικτό

Old age, its physical effects, the sense of horror and the metaphorical knife *are* all the same thing in the poem, and they are all unendurable. Cavafy emphasises this unity of concepts by the interweaving of sound. Such effects can draw attention to less obvious links too. In the opening lines of 'Η συνοδεία του Διονύσου' the harmony of the work of art is reflected in the musical patterning of its subject, <u>sinodia</u> tou <u>Dionisou</u>:

Ο Δάμων ο τεχνίτης (άλλον πιό ικανό
στην Πελοπόννησο δεν έχει) εις παριανό
μάρμαρο επεξεργάζεται την συνοδεία

43

τού Διονύσου. Ο θεός με θεσπεσια
δόξαν εμπρός, με δύναμι στο βάδισμά του.

But consonant δ links the artist Damon, the god Dionysos, the qualities of the god (δόξαν and δύναμι), and the context of the god (συνοδεία and βάδισμα). The poem is as much about the power and glory which the artist is to acquire as about the art work itself, and this musical link between artist and subject matter sets up a subconscious connection before the poem makes it explicit.

3. Language

Despite the controversy over Cavafy's use of 'demotic' and 'katharevousa' forms in his poems (to which I shall refer later in this section), his vocabulary is rarely elaborate or exotic. Instead he prefers to get the full dramatic or emotional effect out of what is largely quite ordinary language. To do this he pays great attention to the choice, placing and combination of words.

Here is a simple example. In 'Ένας γέρος', Cavafy portrays the frustration of an old man pondering on his lost opportunities for pleasure. The contrast is between his misguided inaction in the past and his forced inaction in the present. Now that he recognises the value of giving in to his instincts he is too old to do so. Let us see how the poet's choice of words affects our view of his theme.

The irony of the situation is much strengthened by the role of verbs in the structure of the poem. The framework of the narrative is provided by the first two lines and the last line and a half. These are a grammatical mirror image of one another. In stanza 1 a participular phrase describing a state rather than an action:

Στου καφενείου του βοερού το μέσα μέρος
σκυμένος στο τραπέζι

44

is followed by a verb of motionlessness, κάθετ'. In stanza 6 a verb of motionlessness, αποκοιμάται, is followed by a similar participular phrase:

στου καφενείου ακουμπισμένος το τραπέζι.

Within this framework, which is rather like a 'still' from a film sequence, the action of the poem is entirely mental. Each of the stanzas 2-5 is dominated by a verb of thought in the present tense: σκέπτεται (5), ξέρει (7), συλλογιέται (10), θυμάται (13). Ultimately the action of thought and memory has an intense physical effect on the old man. Hence in line 16 he is dazed not by thoughts and memories but by the *process* of thinking and remembering:

απ' το πολύ να σκέπτεται και να θυμάται
ο γέρος εζαλίσθηκε.

By making his verbs (by definition words of 'action') words of inaction or mental activity, and not physical activity, Cavafy creates the central irony of the poem. In the past the old man truly 'lived' only in his mind. Now, despite his regrets, he is condemned to do the same—and even mental activity is too much for him.

In the above example, what is important is the way in which the grammatical function of a part of speech (the verbs) has been made a part of the 'sense' of the poem. This is only one of a large number of techniques employed by the poet. For practical purposes we can divide them loosely into three groups: word order, choice and stylisation of vocabulary, and register (the combination of forms and words which do not usually appear together in Greek).

3.1 word order

Greek has a much more flexible word order than English, and Cavafy is quick to explore the variety which this provides. Frequently he departs from what would be the normal structure of a sentence in order to emphasise a part of it. A very simple example of this occurs in the first line of 'Εν τω μηνί Αθύρ':

Με δυσκολία διαβάζω   στην πέτρα την αρχαία

where, by using the structure 'definite article, noun, definite article, adjective' popular in folk songs, he can emphasise the word αρχαία, which prepares us for the incompleteness of the inscription which the stone bears. A more interesting example of 'inversion for emphasis' occurs in the last line of 'Δύο νέοι, 23 εως 24 ετών':

στον έρωτα δοθήκαν ευτυχείς.

The poem is a dramatic one, describing a process of miserable waiting which is redeemed by the final appearance of the lover and the mutual pleasure which it brings. By keeping the adjective ευτυχείς to the very end of the last line, Cavafy emphasises that happiness is indeed the climax of the events portrayed.

The resulting word order in the above two examples is not particularly unusual. Emphasis by division and by inversion is a little more striking and consciously poetic. In line 2 of 'Αιμιλιανός Μονάη', for example, Cavafy divides the adjective from its noun entirely:

μια εξαίρετη θα κάμω πανοπλία.

This helps to strengthen an apparently banal adjective. Appropriately so, as the 'armour' is indeed exceptional, since it is metaphorical. Emphasis by inversion is more flexible in its effect, depending on the context. In 'Οταν διεγείρονται' (l.3):

Του ερωτισμού σου τα οράματα

the construction 'genitive + noun it qualifies' merely stresses the reference to love-making. The emphasis is necessary because although the visions are the central subject of the poem, this is the only phrase which defines their nature. But when the same construction is used in the second line of 'Εν πορεία προς την Σινώπην', the description of Mithridates as μεγάλων πόλεων ο κύριος adds a touch of ironic pomposity to the portrait of man mistaken as to his own power. All the examples of non-standard word order which I have given so far have been used for emphasis. Though this is probably its most common function, it is not its only one, or its most subtle one. In the very last line of 'Φωνές', for example, the division

σα μουσική, την νύχτα, μακρυνή, που σβύνει

is for rhythmic and musical effect. The effect can indeed be multiple. In 'Μέρες του 1903' the structure of the repeated phrase

τα ποιητικά τα μάτια, το χλωμό το πρόσωπο

has a number of functions. First, it emphasises the adjectives 'poetic' and 'pale'. Secondly, because it is a construction commonly found in folk-poetry and late nineteenth century lyrics, it helps to activate the meaning of the adjective ποιητικά. Thirdly, it helps to feature the definite article, the point being that, paradoxically, this is a poem about very *indefinite* objects. The constant repetition of 'the' in apparently but deceptively precise references—'the' eyes, 'the' face, 'the' lips—is part of the creation of the sense of an almost lost reality barely grasped by the speaker in the poem and even less accessible to the reader.

C. P. Cavafy

3.2 choice and stylisation of vocabulary

All poets pay great attention to the selection and placing of words. But, as I said above, one of the special characteristics of Cavafy's poetry is that he has relatively little interest in rare words or striking combinations, preferring instead to squeeze the maximum effect out of ordinary vocabulary.

When we looked at ''Ενας γέρος', we saw how Cavafy used the role of the verb as 'action' word in a sentence, and turned the idea on its head to emphasise the forced inaction of old age. This sensitivity to the grammatical categories of words and to the semantic implications of these categories is fundamental to Cavafy's style.

A good place to start, when examining this phenomenon, is a short poem such as 'Η δόξα των Πτολεμαίων'. Here is a poem in which the verbs are almost entirely insignificant—I am, there is, he is. The last two lines have no verb at all. The featured words are nouns: king, possessor, strength, riches, pleasure, luxury, city, summit, language and art. Even the central opposition of the poem is done with nouns—Lagid versus Seleucid, Alexandrian (by implication) versus Macedonian or barbarian. The poem is a hymn to a state of affairs, the power and glory of Alexandria under the Ptolemies. The reason why Cavafy does not, in his opening line, specify which Ptolemy, is precisely because it does not matter which. The supremacy of the city in all that matters in life is simply there, as a given fact. The poet fills his poem with nouns because the static quality of the noun as a part of speech helps to emphasise this sense of permanence.

A more complex variety of the same technique can be found in 'Εκόμισα εις την Τέχνην'. The nouns of 'Η δόξα των Πτολεμαίων', even when they are abstracts (strength, riches, pleasure) all suggest material phenomena—armies, money, physical indulgence. In 'Εκόμισα εις την Τέχνην', on the contrary, the nouns are principally abstracts: desires, feelings, Art, memories, Shape of Beauty, life, impressions, days. Only the references to faces, lines and loves give a more physical association. But this is not to say that the poem is static. On the contrary, it is merely the speaker who is static, as the opening

48

words Κάθομαι και ρεμβάζω show us. All the verbs in the present tense relating to the speaker are words of inaction. It is Art which is the active force, and governs the only verb of real action: Art 'knows how to fashion' beauty. Whereas all the nouns which art works with are ones which suggest past actions—desire, feeling, memory, impressions. The poet's life is now preserved in his art, and this tension between action and state is emphasised by the balance of certain kinds of verb and noun within the poem.

Sometimes Cavafy uses the opposition of lines in which different parts of speech predominate as a way of helping to structure oppositions in the content of the poem. In 'Η αρχή των', for example, the first and last lines are dominated by the nouns—fulfilment, sensual pleasure, verses and beginning. This grammatical balance mirrors a balance in the ideas of the poem (emphasised by the fact that the poem ends on 'beginning'). The fulfilment found in sensual pleasure precisely *is* the beginning of the process by which the verses will come to be written. Lines 2-6, by contrast are full of verbs:

> Απ' το στρώμα σηκωθήκαν,
> και βιαστικά ντύνονται χωρίς να μιλούν.
> Βγαίνουνε χωριστά, κρυφά απ' το σπίτι· και καθώς
> βαδίζουνε κάπως ανήσυχα στον δρόμο, μοιάζει
> σαν να υποψιάζονται πού κάτι επάνω των προδίδει
> σε τι είδους κλίνην έπεσαν προ ολίγου.

They are verbs of action: get up, dress, go out, walk, suspect, betray, go to bed. And they carry with them a whole series of dramatic adverbs and adverbial clauses—without speaking, separately, secretly, uneasily—which in turn link with the verbs of suspicion and betrayal. The first line in the whole poem where verb and noun play an equal part is 7, where 'life' and 'artist' are balanced by 'gained'. In lines 8 and 9:

> Αύριο, μεθαύριο, η μετά χρόνια θα γραφούν

οι στίχ' οι δυνατοί που εδώ ήταν η αρχή των

the balance occurs between the lines—will be written, verses, beginning. This is, of course, the point of the poem. It is only in the artist that the action and its effect are in harmony. The real result of the nouns of line 1 is not the shame-faced nervousness evoked by all the verbs of lines 2-7: it is the poem itself, as declared in line 9.

In a longer poem, the role of grammatical patterns of this sort will obviously be related to other sorts of pattern. In 'Απ' τες Εννιά' we have another poem where verbs are more significant in the verses which frame the poem, while the centre is dominated by nouns. In the first verse, has passed, I lit, I sat, I was sitting; in the last, has passed (twice). The only significant action here is performed by time. As far as the speaker is concerned, the verbs parodoxically emphasise his inactivity:

[...] Κάθουμουν χωρίς να διαβάζω,
και χωρίς να μιλώ.

By contrast the nouns of the central two stanzas, associated with the vision of himself when young, hint at a lost world of action—rooms, sensual pleasure, streets, places of entertainment, theatres, cafes, family mournings, feelings. Grammatically, the richness of past action is now 'frozen' in the procession of nouns: the only verbs 'ήλθε και μ' έφερε' are the actions of a dead self upon the present, inactive self. This ironic reversal of grammatical categories reinforces another pattern. In the first stanza, which is five line long, there are four sentences: in the fourteen lines of stanzas two and three, there are only four sentences too. In the two lines of the last stanza there are another four. So the framework of the poem, dominated by verbs, is grammatically and rhythmically fragmented, whilst the centre, with its elaborate evocation of the past in a series of nouns and noun phrases, is grammatically and rhythmically elaborate. The grammar, syntax and rhythm combine to emphasise the emptiness and stasis of the present and its contrast with the lost fullness of the past.

I have been trying to emphasise that it matters very much in Cavafy what proportion of different parts of speech he uses, what types of noun, what tenses and forms of verb. This is one of his ways of intensifying key meanings and patterns of meaning in the poems. But what about adjectives? Greek poetry in particular is marked by a tradition of elaborate epithets. In Cavafy the most immediately striking feature of the adjectives is, on the contrary, their relative scarcity, and their apparent banality. But it is dangerous to underestimate them.

There are two main functions of the adjective in Cavafy: to describe physical and emotional states—colour, shape, mood—and to intensify themes. He makes sparing use of the first of these functions. Richness, sensuality, decadence, decay can all be 'placed' in a poem by the use of one or two adjectives with clear connotations, evoking a specific atmosphere or set of associations: ebony bed, rose-coloured pearls, heavily-scented rooms, faded cinnamon-coloured suit, melancholy day. A good example of this technique is the line:

Α των γυμνών σωμάτων η ηδονή προ πάντων
('Η διοριά του Νέρωνος')

where the emperor's indifference to his political context and absorption in sensual appetite is crystallised in the adjective 'naked', emphasised by the placing of the genitive phrase 'of naked bodies' before the noun 'ηδονή' which it qualifies. But not all 'physical' adjectives play so simple a role. Sometimes Cavafy overthrows our expectations by deliberately using such words as though they convey something general, in contexts where they do not. Thus, the poems on eyes invoke colours (grey, sapphire, chestnut) which are merely impenetrable surfaces to the reader but which have special power to stimulate in the speaker the memory of a lost past. This strengthens our awareness of the unique nature of a memory, its specificity to the individual remembering it.

His thematic use of adjectives, less conventional and more striking that his descriptive use, is only an extension of the way in which 'naked' is used in the example above. If words such as ideal, beautiful, young, poetic, erotic, sensitive, squalid, pointless, cheap, monotonous recur, it is not for want of imagination on the poet's part. Take, for example, the only adjectives to occur in 'Ζωγραφισμένα', ωραίο and θείο. The poem suggests the powerful effect of beauty on the beholder—especially on the artist. The precise qualities of the boy in the painting are irrelevant. All that counts is the viewer's response to him. The association of 'divine' with 'beautiful' intensifies the sense of an experience which goes beyond the mundane. The adjectives tell us nothing physical about the painting, but they strengthen the abstract argument of the poem. The reverse process, by which an abstract adjective becomes more physical, also occurs in Cavafy's poetry. In 'Μελαγχολία του Ιάσωνος Κλεάνδρου', for example, the only adjective, φρικτό, which occurs twice, does not merely mean 'frightful' in an affected sense; it emphasises the speaker's real fear of growing old.

By focussing on individual adjectives in this way Cavafy, as well as highlighting particular motifs—beauty, sensuality, difference from the norm, arrogance, fear, can also heighten oppositions within a poem (light/dark, beautiful/wretched, even Greek/Barbarian). In 'Μια Νύχτα', for example, an extensive series of words emphasises the negative qualities of the physical context: πτωχική, πρόστυχη, ύποπτη, ακάθαρτο, στενό, λαϊκό, ταπεινό. Two words, ηδονικά and ροδινά, provide the counterbalance, the beauty of the sexual relationship which illuminated the shabby environment. Cavafy repeats 'rosy', using the symbolic associations of the physical detail to evoke the happiness of the moment. The final adjective, μονήρες, is part of another opposition within the poem, the togetherness of the past and the loneliness of the present. But the intensity of the memory has been enough to transcend this gap. The tension between the sets of adjectives is an essential part in the creation of the sense of that intensity.

Because Cavafy gives great weight to a limited range of adjectives, their meaning and importance is coloured by the context in which a reader has met them before. In 'Μέρες του 1908' the first three stanzas have no adjectives at all. In the next three, there is one, negative adjective in each: φρικτό, τρομερό and ξεθωριασμένη. These words characterise the nastiness and squalor of the boy's environment, and this seediness is taken up in the first half of the final stanza, in the reference to the 'unworthy' clothes, the 'mended' underwear. But the final lines oppose a series of words which, in the Cavafean vocabulary have a totally different set of connotations: ολόγυμνος, ωραίος, αχτένιστα and ανασηκωμένα (applied to hair). This might seem to be simply an opposition between squalor and beauty. But the point about the combination of references to beauty, nudity and hair is that they are all marks of *classical* beauty for Cavafy:

> Μαλλιά σαν από αγάλματα ελληνικά παρμένα·
> πάντα έμορφα, κι αχτένιστα σαν είναι
> ('Έτσι πολύ ατένισα')

> (...) έναν ωραίον νεον,
> γυμνόν, ερωτικόν·
> ('Τεχνουργός κρατήρων')

All the adjectives applied to the environment stress the negative qualities of the modern world. All those applied to the boy detach him from that modern world by presenting him in terms of the positive qualities of the ancient world.

An important aspect of Cavafy's 'thematic' use of adjectives is, therefore, an element of verbal stylisation. This stylisation extends, in fact, well beyond any single part of speech. The way in which it is achieved is clear if we look further at his descriptions of young men and his references to erotic encounters. It makes no real difference whether the poems are given historical or modern settings. The young men are not in fact described at all. The reader is merely encouraged to think of them in certain specific terms via a limited number of traits. The 'type'

C. P. Cavafy

is indicated by the word ἔφηβος, which occurs just as much in poems such as 'Μέρες του 1901' as in 'Αριστόβουλος' or 'Θέατρον της Σιδώνος'. The essential qualities of these ἔφηβοι are their youth (frequent references to νέος and to precise ages in the 20s), beauty (έμορφος or ωραίος), and sensitivity (αισθητικός):

Τα έμορφά τους πρόσωπα, τα εξαίσιά τους νειάτα,
η αισθητική αγάπη που είχαν μεταξύ τους
('Δύο νέοι, 23 έως 24 ετών')

(...) Όμως τον θυμούμαι σαν πιο έμορφο.
Μέχρι παθήσεως ήταν αισθητικός.
('Του πλοίου')

There is frequent reference to the body (σώμα) and flesh (σαρξ) but more precise physical references are few, and are still in a general form. The most important are to limbs, lips and eyes; there are rarer references to hands, faces, hair:

Γραμμές του σώματος. Κόκκινα χείλη. Μέλη ηδονικά.
Μαλλιά σαν από αγάλματα ελληνικά παρμένα·
('Έτσι πολύ ατένισα')

These physical references are combined with one or more groups of abstract concepts which are much more important than the physical details themselves: the ideal (ιδανικός, ιδεώδης), pleasure (ηδονή, ηδονικός, έρως, ερωτικός, απόλαυσις), eliteness (έκλεκτος), and eliteness seen from a negative aspect, in the form of the abnormal or forbidden (παράνομος, έκνομος, ανώμαλος). A classic combination of the two sets of references can be found in the last stanza of 'Σ' ένα βιβλίο παληό':

Γιατί ήταν φανερό σαν έβλεπες το έργον

54

(εύκολα νοιώθονταν η ιδέα του καλλιτέχνου)
πού γιά όσους αγαπούνε κάπως υγιεινά,
μες στ' οπωσδήποτε επιτετραμμένον μένοντες,
δεν ήταν προωρισμένος ο έφηβος
της ζωγραφιάς —με καστανά, βαθύχροα μάτια·
με του προσώπου του την εκλεκτή εμορφιά,
την εμορφιά των ανωμάλων έλξεων·
με τα ιδεώδη χείλη του πού φέρνουνε
την ηδονή εις αγαπημένο σώμα·
με τα ιδεώδη μέλη του πλασμένα γιά κρεββάτια
που αναίσχυντα τ' αποκαλεί η τρεχάμενη ηθική.

Wherever such combinations of vocabulary occur, they automatically refer us to Cavafy's particular world view, the privileged position given to youth, beauty, sensuality, and aesthetic sensibility as the characteristics of an elite whose existence is justified by the inspiration which they bring to members of another elite, artists. Cavafy implicitly justifies this stylisation in an interesting way in 'Έτσι πολύ ατένισα' in the phrase

Πρόσωπα της αγάπης, όπως τ'άθελεν
η ποίησις μου.

The poem as a whole describes the way in which reality, memory, dream and art interrelate. The form which both perception and memory take is dictated by what the poet's artistic instinct selects as aesthetically satisfying. Stylisation is a necessary part of the vision itself: verbal stylisation is only the inevitable result.

3.3 register
The most problematic aspect of Cavafy's style is his use of vocabulary, morphology and syntax from different periods of the Greek language.

C. P. Cavafy

Once we get past the early attempts to write entirely in katharevousa, it is hardly possible to speak of a clear division of linguistic form in Cavafy. The evidence of the manuscripts suggests that he started to 'correct' the more conscious katharevousa elements in his writing sometime after 1893, possibly under the influence of the linguistic ideas expressed by Rhoidis in *Τα Είδωλα*. But in many cases not enough is known of educated speech in Constantinople and Alexandria in his day for us to be certain that the use of a given word or form is consciously artificial, and the contemporary commentators on his use of language are usually too bound up themselves in the cultural politics of linguistic forms, or too unskilled as linguists, for their judgments to carry much weight. On the other hand, when a contemporary attributes to Cavafy the view that the Greek language is a continuum which should be studied and used to the full, we have to agree that there is every sign that this is the case. At one end of the spectrum we have his willingness to incorporate extended passages of Ancient Greek into his texts ('Ουκ έγνως, Άγε, ω βασιλεύ Λακεδαιμονίων'). at the other the colloquialisms of 'Ωραία λουλούδια κι άσπρα ως ταίριαζαν πολύ'). Detailed studies of the poems have isolated some dialect peculiarities (the use of the accusative for the genitive in some constructions, for example), just as they have demonstrated a preference for conservative forms of third declension nouns (—is, —i, —eos) and an even more conservative preference for a full system of participles. But these isolated features are of little interest in themselves. They become significant only when there seems to be a particular thematic reason for the preference for a certain sort of language, or where there is a clear linguistic clash.

An example of the simplest sort of effect to be got from a clash of different forms can be found in the last stanza of 'Η δυσαρέσκεια του Σελευκίδου'. The poem has spent two stanzas on the displeasure of Demetrius Soter at the impoverished state in which Ptolemy Philometor has arrived in Rome to present himself as a suppliant before the Roman Senate. The main characters are called by their dynastic titles to stress their position as representatives of the two great Greek royal houses of

56

the post-Alexander period. In the third stanza Ptolemy is shown to
understand the psychology of his position better than Demetrius. He
realises that he needs to play up his role as dependent on the Romans in
every way:

Αλλ' ο Λαγίδης, πού ήλθε γιά την επαιτεία,
ήξερε την δουλειά του και τ' αρνήθηκε όλα·
διόλου δεν του χρειάζονταν αυτές η πολυτέλειες.
Παληοντυμένος, ταπεινός μπήκε στήν Ρώμη,
και κόνεψε σ' ενός μικρού τεχνίτου σπίτι.
Κ' έπειτα παρουσιάσθηκε σαν κακομοίρης
και σαν πτωχάνθρωπος στην Σύγκλητο,
έτοι με πιο αποτέλεσμα να ζητιανέψει.

There are two references to begging here, one at the end of the first line,
επαιτεία, the other at the end of the last, να ζητιανέψει. The first is an
exclusively classical and katharevousa form, the second is plainly
demotic. By ostentatiously supplanting the formal term, with its solemn
stylistic associations, by the colloquial one in this way, Cavafy stresses
Ptolemy's action in rejecting the traditional role of grandiose suppliant
in favour of that of a man humbly begging for assistance. Ptolemy has
come για την επαιτεία but he is deliberately undertaking it in the guise
of a mere ζητιάνος.

An opposition of forms need not mean an opposition of meanings,
however. In the third stanza of 'Μέρες του 1909, '10 και '11', after
evoking the life-style of a poor youth who sells his body for the price of
a tie or a shirt which he fancies, Cavafy makes an overt comparison
between the boy and his classical forerunners:

Διερωτώμαι αν στους αρχαίους καιρούς
είχεν η ένδοξη Αλεξάνδρεια νέον πιό περικαλλή,
πιό τέλειο αγόρι από αυτόν — πού πήε χαμένος:
δεν έγινε, εννοείται, αγαλμά του η ζωγραφιά·

The phrase νέον πιο περικαλλή, with its ostentatiously archaic adjective, is thus juxtaposed with πιο τέλειο αγόρι, a purely demotic phrase. The linguistic differences in the description of a single character emphasise the idea of the boy as a representative, in the modern world, of qualities characteristic in the ancient. His beauty is timeless: the language which describes it bridges the ancient and the modern world.

The role of the register-clashes in the above examples is directly related to a major theme of the poem in which each occurs. But such linguistic oppositions may be part of a more subtle set of contrasts. In 'Ο Βασιλεύς Δημήτριος', the last word of the poem (l.12) is the katharevousa απέρχεται, and it stands in contrast to the other verb for departing, the demotic ξέφυγε at the end of l.9. At first sight it looks very odd to attribute the formal word to the informal action—the actor who changes out of his costume at the end of a performance and slips out of the theatre. But the opposition ξέφυγε/απέρχεται is part of a wider opposition:

> βασιλεύς (king) ... ... ξέφυγε
> ηθοποιός (actor) ... ... απέρχεται

The fact that the king changes roles with the actor is mirrored in the exchange katharevousa noun + demotic verb / demotic noun + katharevousa verb.

These three examples look at the effects to be got from individual pairs of words. But often in Cavafy patterning is much more extensive. One of the most notorious mixtures of forms occurs in the rhymes of 'Τείχη'. It is also an excellent example of how careful such a mixture can in fact be.

> Χωρίς περίσκεψιν, χωρίς λύπην, χωρίς αιδώ
> μεγάλα κ' υψηλά τριγύρω μου εκτισαν τείχη.

> Και κάθομαι και απελπίζομαι τώρα εδώ.

Ἄλλο δεν σκέπτομαι: τον νούν μου τρώγει αυτή η τύχη·

διότι πράγματα πολλά έξω να κάμω είχον.

Α όταν έκτιζαν τα τείχη πώς να μην προσέξω.

Αλλά δεν άκουσα ποτέ κρότον κτιστών η ήχον.

Ανεπαισθήτως μ᾽ έκλεισαν από τον κόσμον έξω.

All the rhymes but one in this poem are 'equivocal': they consist of pairs of words which sound identical in every respect but are completely different: 'shame' and 'here', 'walls' and 'fate', 'I had' and 'sound'. In each of these equivocal rhymes, the first word is a katharevousa form or usage, the second a demotic form (or at least, in the case of ήχος a neutral one). In the first two stanzas this opposition between forms follows the thematic opposition between the 'I' who speaks the poem and the 'they' who are walling him in. 'Without shame' and 'walls' are aspects of 'them'; 'here' and 'fate' are aspects of 'I'. In the third pair the relationship katharevousa / demotic = they / I appears reversed. 'I had' describes the self as it would have been in the lost world outside the walls; the absence of 'noise' is a comment on the actions of 'them'. In fact, however, this third pair modifies the opposition I / they: what is really being contrasted in lines 1-4 and 5 and 7 is not so much two people or groups of people as two worlds, *outside* and *inside*. Hence the katharevousa rhyme represents what 'I' would have done outside, the demotic one the silence which prevails inside. But the most striking rhyme is the fourth one, 'pay attention' and 'outside', precisely because it is the only one in which two demotic forms are matched. Now προσέξω contains an element of punning. In l.5 the poet has already used έξω = outside, so that the reader naturally divides into προς έξω = towards the outside—where the speaker should have directed his attention, and where he wants to go. This punning effect is then strengthened by actually rhyming προσέξω with έξω. The katharevousa / demotic rhymes establish the hopeless desire for the outer. Cavafy has used the register difference of demotic and katharevousa to pattern his rhyme words in such a way as to emphasise both the sense of division and the consequent overpowering yearning for the lost outside world.

4. Structural patterning

In everything I have said so far about Cavafy's poetic vision and his poetic manner, I have constantly referred to patterns. The most basic of these is the simple opposition: Christian and pagan, Greek and barbarian, old age and youth, beauty and squalor, intention and achievement, ancient world and modern. Such oppositions can, as we have seen, be formal as much as thematic: different rhymes, predominance of different parts of speech, different linguistic registers. It is these oppositions which form the basis of structural patterns which are fundamental to the way in which poems affect us.

A good example of how complex patterning works can be found in 'Ὁ καθρέπτης στην εἴσοδο', a poem which at first sight seems so simple as to be almost unpoetic:

Το πλούσιο σπίτι είχε στην είσοδο
έναν καθρέπτη μέγιστο, πολύ παλαιό·
τουλάχιστον προ ογδόντα ετών αγορασμένο.

Ένα εμορφότατο παιδι, υπάλληλος σε ράπτη
(τες Κυριακές, ερασιτέχνης αθλητής),
στέκονταν μ' ένα δέμα. Το παρέδοσε
σε κάποιον του σπιτιού, κι αυτός το πήγε μέσα
να φέρει την απόδειξι. Ο υπάλληλος του ράπτη
έμεινε μόνος, και περίμενε.
Πλησίασε στον καθρέπτη και κυττάζονταν
κ' έσιαζε την κραβάτα του. Μετά πέντε λεπτά
του φέραν την απόδειξι. Την πήρε κ έφυγε.

Μα ο παλαιός καθρέπτης πού είχε δεί και δεί,
κατα την υπαρξίν του την πολυετή,
χιλιάδες πράγματα και πρόσωπα·
μα ο παλαιός καθρέπτης τώρα χαίρονταν,
κ' επαίρονταν πού είχε δεχθεί επάνω του
την άρτιαν εμορφιά γιά μερικά λεπτά.

The poem is in three sections. A (3 lines) and C (6 lines) are devoted to the mirror, B (9 lines) is devoted to the tailor's employee. The structure is thus that of a framework around a narrative—an insignificant incident in which a boy delivers a parcel, stops to look at himself in the mirror, then goes away.

In section A, the first part of the frame of the poem, the mirror starts as an object, literally and grammatically, since it is the possession of the wealthy house. But in the second part of the frame (C), after the boy has looked into the mirror, it comes to life:

μα ο παλαιός καθρέπτης τώρα χαίρονταν,
κ' επαίρονταν που είχε δεχθεί επάνω του
την άρτιαν εμορφιά για μερικά λεπτά.

Its passive quality is modified: it 'has received <the boy's reflection> upon itself'. On the other hand the boy, who is the active agent of the narrative in the middle section of the poem (B), becomes momentarily passive when he sees himself reflected in the mirror (κυττάζονταν is reflexive in meaning but passive in form).

The opposition, momentarily transcended, between the mirror and the boy is also an opposition in time. The mirror occupies a band of time (eighty years in frame A, emphasised by πολυετή in frame C), but the boy is transitory. The fact that their encounter takes place in a hall-way emphasises the transitoriness: entrances are places for casual encounters (usually erotic) in Cavafy's poems. However, the boy's beauty is assimilated into the mirror's memory, and thereby is incorporated into a wider spectrum of time. The mirror is credited with the capacity usually reserved for art, or at least for the artist, of preserving fugitive moments.

These thematic patterns are sustained by stylistic ones. The two subjects, the mirror and the boy, have a musical connexion: ipallilos t<ou> ra<f>ti and pal<e>os ka<th>r<e>ptis contain a large number of the same sounds in a different sequence, and in the case of f and th both belong to the same class of sound (fricative). There are also structural parallels in the way in which the two are introduced. Each is prefaced by the indefinite article—ἕναν καθρέπτη, ἕνα παιδί. Each is qualified by a superlative adjective—μέγιστο, εμορφότατο; each is also qualified by a parenthesis, a secondary descriptive phrase. And these phrases are characteristic of their protagonists. Line 3 expands upon a known quality of the mirror, stressing its permanence. Line 5 offers a random, disconnected quality of the boy, exemplifying his transience. His only permanent characteristic in the context of the poem is his beauty. Even the syntax and rhythm emphasise the parallel between mirror and boy, since neither introduction contains any enjambement, although the B section of the poem is full of it.

So far I have mainly dealt with the frame sections, A and C. The narrative structure in B is itself an inverted image of the overall shape of the poem. Το παρέδοσε ... την απόδειξι = action, Ο υπάλληλος ... κραβάτα του = reflection, and Μετά πέντε λεπτά ... έφυγε = action. But this time the transient elements (represented by the aorist verb forms) are the framework and the lasting ones (represented by the verbs which are durative in form and/or sense) are the centre. At the key point in the text where mirror and boy come together, everything in the boy's actions is musically linked to the mirror. Even if we simply take the key words καθρέπτη, κυττάζονταν and κραβάτα the link is obvious. It becomes more striking if we look at ll. 10-11 in detail. I have listed the sounds of στον καθρέπτη vertically, and their appearance in words relating to the boy horizontally:

s   πλησίασε, έσιαζε
t   κυττάζονταν, την, κραβάτα, του
on   κυττάζονταν + other nasals
(n)k την κραβάτα + (without the nasal) και, κυττάζονταν
a   πλησίασε, κυττάζονταν, έσιαζε, κραβάτα
\<th\> \<no equivalents\>
r   κραβάτα
e   πλησίασε, και, έσιαζε
p   πλησίασε
t   (see above)
i   πλησίασε

Cavafy has taken a banal incident, and with truly baroque bravura, has woven a web of parallels and oppositions, at the centre of which is a moment of physical identification of subject (boy) and object (mirror)—the boy's reflection in the mirror—which is at the same time a moment of concentrated musical identification between the words describing subject and object. The poem offers, perhaps, an extreme example of patterning, but one which can open our eyes to similar techniques throughout Cavafy's work.

PART III: EIGHT COMMENTARIES

Poetic techniques take their effect from their context. Now that we have looked at a wide range of types of technique to be found in Cavafy's work, let us examine a number of poems in depth, to see how their overall 'meaning' is not just a question of content but is governed by the way in which they are written. A word of warning. None of these readings can be definitive, or even exhaustive. In some, such as 'Εν απογνώσει', I shall pay minute attention to verse form and musical patterns; in others, particularly 'Μύρης· Αλεξάνδρεια του 340 M.X.' I shall pay more attention to thematic patterns and narrative perspective. The focus will change in accordance with my view of what the major features governing the effect of each individual poem are. But in all of them I shall try to show that form creates, controls and changes meaning.

As for the choice of texts: Cavafy is an unexpectedly varied writer, for a man whose thematic range is ostensibly narrow. I have not been able, in the space available, to cover examples of his whole range, either of theme or of form: I have not, for example, included an epitaph or any of the short poems on the nature of poetic experience. But I have consciously included long and short poems, rhymed and unrhymed poems, modern and classical settings, 3rd person narratives and dramatic monologues. My principal aim has been to select a sufficient range of poems to give some idea of the characteristic qualities of Cavafy's writing and at the same time show that similarity of theme or similarity of form does not, in the end, produce similar poems.

1
ΕΝ ΑΠΟΓΝΩΣΕΙ
In Desperation

Τον έχασ' εντελώς.   Και τώρα πιά ζητεί
στα χείλη καθενός   καινούριου εραστή
τα χείλη τα δικά του·   στην ένωσι με κάθε
καινούριον εραστή   ζητεί να πλανηθεί
πώς είναι ο ίδιος νέος.   πώς δίδεται σ' εκείνον.

Τον εχασ' εντελώς,   σαν να μη υπήρχε καν.
Γιατί ήθελε — ειπ' εκείνος —   ήθελε να σωθεί
απ την στιγματισμένη,   την νοσηρά ηδονή·
απ' την στιγματισμένη,   του αίσχους ηδονή.
Ήταν καιρός ακόμη —   ως είπε — να σωθεί.

Τον έχασ' εντελώς,   σαν να μη υπήρχε καν.
Από την φαντασίαν,   από τες παραισθήσεις
στα χείλη άλλων νέων   τα χείλη του ζητεί·
γυρεύει να αισθανθεί   ξανά τον ερωτά του.

In this poem Cavafy explores the effect on the beloved of the loss of his lover. (For ease of reference I will call them, respectively, A and B.) Neither boy is given a physical presence or a social context, and there is no sense of individual personality. Indeed, the sex of A has to be guessed from the references to sick and shameless love in the second stanza. All incidental detail has been omitted, leaving a poem about the deep emotional effects of a sexual relationship. Nevertheless, it is not a sensual poem. There is no physical vocabulary except *lips*, the part of the body which carries connotations of both physical (kissing) and verbal communication. This fits well with the choice of the noun ένωσι (union) for the sexual act in 1.3. The abandoned lover is looking for something more than physical sex; he wants to rediscover an emotional communion now lost. But the lips of other boys are merely an instrument of sensual

65

exchange. So the poem is as much an expression of loss as of despair. The intensity of this sense of loss is in part because it is the loss of the past as well as of the present/future: 'He had lost him completely, as though he had never existed' (1.6). This sounds like a cliché. But the following lines spell out how the past has been psychologically destroyed by B's negative view of the love affair. He consciously rejected the affair by adopting society's hostile evaluation of it (στιγματισμένη, νοσηρά, του αίσχους), and implied that their love was a destructive force by contrasting it with 'salvation'. The loss of the past is a loss of part of the self. A's desperate attempt to delude himself that the love may be recoverable is not an attempt to find his lover in any literal sense, but to find everything his lover stood for and thereby to re-instate his own lost 'self'. Note the ambiguity of two key half-lines. In 1.5, πώς είναι ο ίδιος νέος means both that A wants to deceive himself that every boy he is with is his lost lover, and also that he wants to believe that he himself is the same as he was before the break-up. In the final phrase 'he is seeking to feel his love again' (1.14) the του applies to both the beloved and the lost lover. He wants to give and receive the same love as before.

The title of the poem is significant. Απόγνωσις has the etymological sense of 'giving up', 'abandoning', as well as the current meaning, desperation. So that at one level the title defines the position of both the two lovers. One has abandoned the other, and the abandoned lover is in despair. At another level, it points to the fact that what dominates the poem is *the abandoning of the self* to despair, the frenzy of desperation. Abstract ideas of this sort need considerable skill to translate them into poetically effective terms. Let us see how Cavafy has tackled the problem.

The most obvious formal feature of the poem is repetition. The regularity of the rhythmic structure helps to make the various kinds of repetition stand out. All the lines are divided into two roughly equal parts. The half lines are basically iambic trimeters: most of them have two stresses in each, and a total of six or seven, syllables. So the poet has, not fourteen lines, but twenty eight half-lines in which he can create echoes and patterns of sense, sound and structure.

The first group of repetitions which strike the reader is made up of entire half-lines: 1a = 6a = 11a: 6b = 11b. These lines, which also stand out physically on the page because they each begin a stanza, contain two of the key ideas of the poem, A's total loss of B, and the annihilation of the past. The other repeated half-line, 8a = 9a, emphasises B's rejection of their love and his acceptance of society's condemnation of it. There is a fourth half-line which recurs in an almost identical form: 2b/4a. This is the last of the key ideas—the recurrence of new lovers—and its appearance in a form almost, but not quite, identical is itself a marker of the status of the new lovers in the poem, for they too are similar to, but not the same as, what has been lost.

Tied in with this is a set of repetitions with variation, four half-lines in which *lips* occur: 2a = 3a = 13a = 13b (13b is also a repetition of ζητεί from 1b, see below). Here the sole physical image of the poem, symbolising communication of both mind and body, is applied to both what has been lost (the lips of B in 3a, 13b) and to the attempt to rediscover or recreate what has been lost (the lips of the succession of new lovers in 2a, 13a). Finally, certain key ideas are emphasised by the repetition of individual words or short phrases: the beloved's search (ζητεί 1a, 4b, 13b), the contrasting desire of the lover (ήθελε 7a, 7b), the idea that the rejection of their love would be a way of being saved (να σωθεί 7b, 10b), the important element of sensual pleasure (ηδονή 8b, 9b).

This might seem quite enough repetition for a short poem. But I have only scratched the surface. So far we have seen how repetitions emphasise themes and evoke the repetitious nature of the experiences undergone. Backing up the repetition of words and phrases are repetitions of grammatical structures: 5a and b contain two parallel πώς clauses; 12a, 12b two parallel από + noun phrases; 4b, 6b, 14a three equivalent verb + να + verb constructions (where the first verbs are all of desire or attempt). All these grammatical repetitions help to show equivalences between the different clauses. Note in particular the effect

C. P. Cavafy

of the repetition is lines 8 and 9. Repetition of the words themselves helps to establish the urgent quality of B's desire to escape and the brutality of the way in which he echoes society's view of the love he is rejecting. But the choice of exactly parallel structures has the further effect of making 'sickly' and 'shameful' equivalent. What society disapproves of is automatically unhealthy.

Phrases and structures may be what strike us consciously in the poem when we look for repetitions. But what is likely to strike us unconsciously is musical repetition. 'Εν απογνώσει' is full of it. Although the poem does not have regular rhyme, it uses strong musical patterns at the ends of both lines and half-lines. It begins with a full rhyme drawing our attention to the relationship between two of the key words, ζητεί and εραστή, the frenzied search and the object of the search. At line end, the vowel -i then becomes the link between words which belong to different themes of the poem: πλανηθεί and παραισθήσεις (delusion), ηδονή / σωθεί (sensual pleasure contrasted with salvation), with ζητεί bringing back the theme of the search in l.13. The half-lines have a pattern in -os, linking the 'identity' words: every, he, young man, to the emphatically repeated 'totally'. Twice there are rhymes between half-line and line end, each time using the vowel -i and linking major themes: lover and delusion in l.4, seeking and feeling in 13b/14a. Every word picked out by these musical patterns gains in importance: we are more immediately aware of its role in the line, and the patterns create new relationships with words in other lines. This effect is heightened if we look at other sorts of musical pattern which interweave with the ones already identified. In lines 1-4, for example, the -i sound links ζητεί / χείλη / εραστή / χείλη / εραστή / ζητεί, with πλανηθεί coming at the climax of this musical group: this strengthens the connection between the themes of search and self-delusion.

In fact, the more one looks for musical links between words which have some thematic link, the more one finds. Some one-off patterns occur, e.g. ένωσι / νέος, εκείνος / νοσηρά, but they interlink with others which extend right through the poem: (en) ένωσι, νέος, καθενός,

68

καινούριου, καινούριον; (k)καθενός, καινούριου, δικά, κάθε, εκείνον, etc. After a while the effect is hypnotic. Nothing in the poem is aurally new, and yet nothing is quite the same, just as the vocabulary of desire, sensuality and delusion recurs in ever-changing combinations. When the poet wants to be quite sure of making a word stand out, he sometimes uses the rhythm. Thus he establishes the feeling of feverish promiscuity essential to the mood of the poem by twice using enjambement (at line-end and across the break in the half lines) to give stress to otherwise colourless words: 1.2 καθενός, 1.3 κάθε. Another way of featuring similarly neutral words connected with identity is to put them at rhythmic breaks: δικά του (1.3a) εκείνον (1.5b), εκείνος (1.7a). The more Cavafy emphasises such 'identity words', the less clear we become as to who is who, and the more completely identity breaks down.

Rather than explore his themes of loss and despair through metaphor or highly coloured language, Cavafy has preferred to reproduce the sense of obsession and emotional turmoil in the repetition of words, phrases, sounds and structures, evoking an orgy of anonymous sexuality in which what is sought (love and the self through the rediscovery of the lover) is an impossible goal. The overall effect is of disintegration, total loss of control, with the resulting irony that the search for salvation through the lover is the cause of the gradual destruction of the beloved.

2
ΜΕΣΑ ΣΤΑ ΚΑΠΗΛΕΙΑ
In the Taverns

Μέσα στα καπηλειά   και τα χαμαιτυπεία
της Βηρυτού κυλιέμαι.   Δεν ήθελα να μένω
στην Αλεξάνδρεια εγώ.   Μ' άφισεν ο Ταμίδης·
κ' επήγε με του Επάρχου   τον υιό γιά ν' αποκτήσει
μια έπαυλι στον Νείλο,   ένα μέγαρον στην πόλιν.
Δεν έκανε να μένω   στην Αλεξάνδρεια εγώ. —
Μέσα στα καπηλειά   και τα χαμαιτυπεία
της Βηρυτού κυλιέμαι.   Μες σ' ευτελή κραιπάλη
διάγω ποταπώς.   Το μόνο που με σώζει
σαν εμορφιά διαρκής.   σαν άρωμα πού επάνω
στην σάρκα μου έχει μείνει,   είναι πού είχα δυό χρόνια
δικό μου τον Ταμίδη,   τον πιό εξαίσιο νέο,
δικό μου όχι γιά σπίτι   η για έπαυλι στον Νείλο.

This poem can be grouped with 'Εν απογνώσει', in that it is also about
lost love, uses repetition and is metrically similar. But there are
significant thematic and subtle stylistic differences between the two
poems. Unlike 'Εν απογνώσει', 'Μέσα στα καπηλειά' is rich in
details of place and personality, particularly the personality of the lost
lover Tamides, who has run off the with son of the Prefect. It is
significant that we know a lot about Tamides and nothing much about the
shadowy speaker. Tamides is 'someone', with a smart country villa on
the Nile and a big house in town: the speaker is just another representative of the faceless debauchery of a Middle-Eastern city.

The contrast between the present status of the two boys is neatly
brought out by the placing of Beirut and Alexandria in identical positions

70

in adjacent lines. In the Cavafean world, to exchange Alexandria for Beirut can only be a decline. But at least the break between the lovers has not been marred by remorse. Tamides has gone not because he wants to save himself, but because he can make more out of his new lover. His departure may have destroyed the present and the future, but it has left the past untouched.

The poem is thus divided between a sense of separation and loss, coupled with emphasis on the abject nature of the speaker's present life, and a sense of rejoicing in the beauty of the past. Whereas in 'Εν απογνώσει' the past was sacrificed in order that one lover should be 'saved', here it is the past itself which saves—notice the stress on σώζει at line-end. And it is a past in which sensuality is uppermost: together with an abstract definition of the memory of their love (like eternal beauty) Cavafy gives us a very physical image of it remaining like a scent on the speaker's flesh. Indeed, it is natural to read σαν here as meaning, not 'like' but 'in its role as', so strong is the physical nature of the memory and so effective its power to protect the speaker from his present. Thus what starts as a poem about rejection, ends as an affirmation of the speaker's faith in the value of passion for passion's sake and of the memory of such a passion as giving lasting value to life, however degenerate.

Not surprisingly, then, there is no trace of the frenzy which characterises 'Εν απογνώσει'. In the first part of the poem the tone is more one of muted hopelessness. The main characteristic of the speaker is passivity, a fatalistic submission to his situation. This passivity is reflected in the fact that the more important verbs are in the reflexive or have the speaker as their object rather than their subject: κυλιέμαι, μ'άφισεν, με σώζει. Other verbs tend to be purely verbs of 'existing' (διάγω) or of some other state (έκανε, ήθελα), rather than expressing action. This sense of fatality haunts many of Cavafy's 'lost' young men, e.g. the central character of 'Ένας νέος, της Τέχνης του Λόγου — στο 24ον έτος του'.

If the tone which immediately strikes the reader is one of resignation, the formal effect which first strikes the eye is the repetition of lines

1 and 2a at 7 and 8a. In effect this divides the poem in half, since, as we shall see, it is really a 12 line poem in which the thirteenth line is a variation on the twelfth, like a phrase extension or coda in music. The sense of a break at the end of line 6 is confirmed musically by the fact that it is the only line so far (and in fact the only line in the poem) to end on a stressed syllable, ἐγώ. The subsequent repetition of an entire line and a half then gives the impression of completely restarting the poem, and heavily emphasises the idea of the debauchery into which the speaker has now sunk. But this is by no means the only repetition in the first part of the poem. Within the first six lines: 6a is a variation on 2b, and 6b repeats 3a, emphasising the fact that the end of the affair has driven the speaker from Alexandria. This creates another circular thematic structure overlapping the division into halves:

A: I spend all my time in taverns and brothels
B: I had to get out of Alexandria
C: Tamides left me for mercenary reasons
B: I had to get out of Alexandria
A: I spend all my time in taverns and brothels

The repetition of 1 and 2a as 7 and 8a thus both rounds off one thematic structure and starts another. This pattern suggests a vicious circle of degenerate experience from which the speaker appears unable to escape and in which he passively wallows. But he does escape, to a certain extent, in the second half of the poem. He escapes into memory. The only repetition in this half is the scornful second reference to the villa on the Nile with which the poem closes. Tamides' present life, the central theme (C) of 1-8a, is contrasted with his past as the speaker's lover, and the past wins. There is something triumphant about the placing of δικό μου at the beginning of line 12, emphasised by the preceding enjambement, and this triumph is underlined by the repetition of the same phrase at the beginning of line 13. As I said above, the last line is a musical variation on the preceding one. Structurally the poem has finished, but thematically, this is the punch line. The tone is heightened by the sarcastic replacement of the grandiose μέγαρον of 1.5 by the down-to-earth σπίτι. Tamides has not got such a big deal out of the Prefect's son: bricks and mortar are no substitute for passion. The beauty of his affair with the speaker was that it was a love affair pure and simple, untarnished by anything mercenary. Even after he has been abandoned by Tamides, the speaker can still think of him in idealising terms him as ἐξαίσιο. The glossing of 1.12 by 1.13 sums up for us why the very sensual memory of their affair has the power to last.

If repetition is the first thing to strike the reader, then enjambement must be the second. There are enjambements between lines 1-2, 2-3, 4-5, 7-8, 8-9, 10-11, and 11-12, and similar breaks of the grammatical unit across the central line-break in lines 4 and 6. This wealth of enjambement is rhythmically very disturbing, creating a sense of endless restlessness. It also gives enormous emphasis to those points where the end of the grammatical unit *does* coincide with line end. The first place where the rhythm and grammar come to a halt together is at the end of line 3, after Μ' ἄφισεν ο Ταμίδης. And there are only two other such moments before the close of the poem: one in line 5 (after T's reasons for leaving him) and the second in line 6 (his own need to go elsewhere), where it ends the ABCBA thematic structure analysed above. Thus the few total rhythmic breaks coincide exactly with the stages in the account of the break up of the relationship: theme is mirrored in verse form.

The ancillary effects which Cavafy uses to bring out the elements in the structure which I have defined are many and varied. One device is to exploit the patterns of opposition which the divided metre offers. The separation of the speaker from Tamides, for example, is neatly represented by the placing of εγώ at the central line-break in 3a and Tamides at the end of 3b. The division is then re-emphasised by the parallel between Tamides at the end of 3b and εγώ at the end of 6b. Another device is to emphasise the relationship between words by their positioning and sound. In 1a and 2a two trisyllabic words, kapilya / and kilyeme, are paired in this way and in 7a, 8a and 8b, the same pair occurs again, extended by krep<u>ali</u>. The musical relationship between the words of this set draws attention to them as representing the three key aspects of the speaker's present life: taverns, wallowing, debauchery. Yet another device is to use the difference between trailing and stressed endings at the half-line. In the first six lines only 1.1 καπηλειά and 1.3 ἐγώ end in a stressed syllable at the central line-break, making another small link between the speaker and his lifestyle. In the second half of the poem only 1.9 ποταπώς and 1.10 διαρκής have the stress in this position. Here the rhythmic link stresses contrast rather than connection. The baseness of the speaker's ephemeral present life is redeemed only by the lasting quality of the beauty which his past love has left with him.

3

ΕΝΑΣ ΝΕΟΣ, ΤΗΣ ΤΕΧΝΗΣ ΤΟΥ ΛΟΓΟΥ —ΣΤΟ 24ΟΝ ΕΤΟΣ ΤΟΥ

A young man skilled in the art of the word—in his 24th year.

Όπως μπορείς πιά δούλεψε, μυαλό. —
Τον φθείρει αυτόν μιά απόλαυσις μισή.
Είναι σε μιά κατάστασι εκνευριστική.
Φιλεί το πρόσωπο το αγαπημένο κάθε μέρα,
το χέρια του είναι πάνω στα πιό εξαίσια μέλη.
Ποτέ του δεν αγάπησε με τόσο μέγα
πάθος. Μα λείπει η ωραία πραγμάτωσις
του έρωτος· λείπει η πραγμάτωσις
πού πρέπει νάναι απ' τους δυό μ' έντασιν επιθυμητή.

(Δεν είν' ομοίως δοσμένοι στην ανώμαλη ηδονή κ' οι δυό.
Μονάχ' αυτόν κυρίεψε απολύτως).

Και φθείρεται, και νεύριασε εντελώς.
Εξ άλλου είναι κι άεργος· κι αυτό πολύ συντείνει.
Κάτι μικρά χρηματικά ποσά
με δυσκολία δανείζεται (σχεδόν
τα ζητιανεύει κάποτε) και ψευτοσυντηρείται.
Φιλεί τα λατρεμένα χείλη· πάνω
στο εξαίσιο σώμα — πού όμως τώρα νοιώθει
πώς στέργει μόνον — ηδονίζεται.
Κ' έπειτα πίνει και καπνίζει· πίνει και καπνίζει·
και σέρνεται στα καφενεία ολημερίς,
σέρνει με ανία της εμορφιάς του το μαράζι. —
Όπως μπορείς πιά δούλεψε, μυαλό.

This is a poem describing the effect of a passion which is not fully returned. The young man clearly has a sexual relationship with his lover, but it is neither physically nor emotionally fulfilling, because their commitment to each other is unequal. But though the poem 'tells a story' up to a point, it is not really a narrative poem. The two young men are nameless (I shall refer to them as A and B), they are given no individual physical portrait and no specific physical context. Nothing really happens. The focus of the content of the poem is entirely psychological. It evokes the torment and gradual destructiveness of a relationship in which there is an indefinable separation, a duality where there should be unity. At least, this analysis fits lines 2-22 of the poem. The nature and effect of the first and last lines, and the relationship of the text to the title, I shall look at later.

What strikes one on a first reading of the poem is the passivity of both lover and beloved, though that passivity is conveyed in different ways. B is definitely an object, a face that is kissed (4), limbs that submit to A's hands (5), lips that are kissed (17), an exquisite body (18). The only active verb describing B—and its subject is not B himself but his body—is στέργει (consents) in l.19, a grudgingly passive verb accepting the sexual attentions of A. There is something deliberately distasteful about this sense of one partner allowing another to relieve his sexual instincts on his body (the preposition 'on', in the form πάνω στο, is twice used in this context, in ll.5 and 17-19) without reciprocating. The fact that the two partners are both male has little to do with our distaste: it is the sense of dehumanisation involved which is distressing—and doubly distressing here to A, who wants something more from the relationship.

B, then, is reduced to the status of an erotic object. A's passivity is a more intangible element. He is introduced as the victim of an abstract noun:

Τον φθείρει αυτόν μια απόλαυσις μιση

and this sense of being on the receiving end of a force which he cannot control is repeated in the impersonal construction of 7-9, in 1.11, in φθείρεται (12). Note also the large number of verbs applied to A in 15-23 which are passive in form though reflexive in meaning: δανείζεται, ψευτοσυντηρείται, ηδονίζεται, σέρνεται. It is true that there are plenty of active verbs describing him too, but they are virtually all either connected with his unsuccessful sexuality—4 φιλεί, 6 αγάπησε, 17 φιλεί, with his emotional states 12 νεύριασε, 18 νοιώθει, or (ll.16-23) describe repeated trivial everyday actions, borrowing money, drinking and smoking. The only exception is the forceful metaphor at the climax of the poem in 1.22, σέρνει με ανία της εμορφιάς του το μαράζι. But this is an exception which proves the rule, for it dramatises the state of lifelessness into which he has descended.

So far I have defined the subject of the poem as a singularly static one. Yet it contrives in fact to present a quite dramatic effect. How is this achieved? The answer is, by extremely skilful technical contrivance. In the first place Cavafy uses the lay-out of the poem on the page to produce a three-part structure: the situation, its cause. its effect. Within this structure, he uses the rhythm and sound effects to create significant patterns and emphases. The basic unit of rhythm is iambic, with variation of end-stress: ultimate (a), penultimate (b) and antepenultimate (c). To some extent he plays the length of one line off against the length of the next in order to stress certain words. Thus, in 1.3 εκνευριστική stands out simply because 1.3 is longer and rhythmically different from lines 1 and 2, which have an almost identical five-stress pattern, reinforced by the musical similarity of the second half of the two lines:

(...) πιά δούλεψε, μυαλό
(...) μιά απόλαυσις μισή.

More subtly, Cavafy creates relationships between lines through the pattern of the stresses on end-words. In the first section the pattern is a, a, a, b, b, b, c, c, a. Even where the rhythmic importance of the end word is changed by enjambement (6-7 and 7-8) the words to which these

77

enjambements lead maintain the pattern by reproducing the stress of the words at line end: μέγα / πάθος, πραγμάτωσις / του έρωτος. Though there is no rhyme, this helps to build a progressive structure which falls back on itself, drawing attention to the contrast between the intense shared desire described on the 'a' rhythm at the end of l.9, and the words denoting inadequacy and frustration used on the 'a' rhythm in lines 2 and 3. There are other patterns which also involve the end words. Lines 1,2,4,5 and 6 all end in a two-syllable noun beginning with m, while 9 ends in an adjective whose penultimate syllable also begins in m: 4, 5 and 6 are more closely linked through assonance μέρα / μέλη / μέγα, and indeed 4 and 6 show an even closer relationship between the sounds of equivalent syllables:

αγαπημένο κάθε μέρα
αγάπησε με τόσο μέγα

At the same time, in lines 2-5 grammatical unit and the line coincide, whereas 6 produces both the first enjambement and the first declaration of what is wrong with the relationship.

Overall, the music of the first section is torn between effects of harmony and disharmony. As we move from the positive elements of A's relationship with B to what is lacking, the verse moves from a to b to c stress patterns, from coincidence of grammatical unit and line end to enjambement (at the same time emphasising the words πάθος and έρωτος), from the regular musical system of μέρα / μέλη / μέγα to the first end-words with no m in the appropriate position. All this dramatises the appearance of the explanation: Μα λείπει η ωραία πραγμάτωσις/ του έρωτος, which is then re-emphasised by the repetition of the key word πραγμάτωσις.

The idea of disharmony is made explicit in both the form and the words of the parenthesis which is the central section, the long rhythmically awkward l.10 and the short l.11 with its stress on 'entirely'. The opposition unity/duality is exemplified structurally by contrasting οι δυό at line end with Μονάχ' αυτόν at the beginning of the following line. The third stanza can only repeat the effect already used: a mixture of regular and irregular rhythms, of end-stopped lines and enjambements. The only end-word stressed on the antepenultimate syllable, ηδονίζεται (19), recalls by contrast the word on the equivalent rhythm in the first section, πραγμάτωσις (7 and 8): πραγμάτωσις is what A vainly desires; short-lived sexual pleasure is all he gets. Similarly, the circularity of the life style is conveyed in the repetition, with variation, of ideas and phrases from ll.4-5 in 17-19. We are now aware that everything about the lover's position is excessive, whether it be the idealising language applied to B (εξαίσιος twice, λατρεμένος) or the unrestrained quality of his emotions and actions as represented by the stressed adverbs—11 απολύτως, 12 εντελώς, 21 ολημερίς. The completeness of his passion is thus matched by the completeness of his *ennui*. And just at the end, in the striking image της εμορφιάς του το μαράζι, there is a hint of the value of what is being lost in this tragic mismatch.

As I intimated at the beginning of this analysis, ll.2-22 form an apparently coherent poem in themselves, evoking the waste and frustration of an unfulfilling love-affair. This obliges us to explain both the title and the first and last lines. The title might encourage us to assume that the lover who is the subject of the poem is a writer, though in 2-22 there is no mention of anything beyond his sexual obsession. But lines 1 and 23 are framed in a completely separate grammatical voice, an implied 1st person addressing his own brain. The narrative is in the third person, in present sequence: it does not in itself readily allow us to accept the voice behind the imperative as the voice of A. In any case, what does line 1 mean? An exhortation to the brain to keep working as best it can could, out of context, be interpreted in any number of ways. Yet, despite this disparity of grammatical voices, the formal (rhythmic and musical) unity of the first and last lines with the rest of the poem, and the evident degree of potential overlap between a young man of twenty-four and the subject of the poem, encourage one to feel that it is best to take the three 'characters'—the writer mentioned in the title, the voice issuing the instruction in lines 1 and 23, and the lover—as the same person.

Here is a possible reading which does so. The poem represents the writer's attempt (i.e. the attempt of the writer in the title, since we do not need to get mixed up with the details of Cavafy's own life) to escape from the stultifying effect of an unsatisfying love-affair by projecting his experience in the third person. He objectifies his emotional problems and subordinates them to the aesthetic problems of writing. The mental block induced by his sexual obsession is thus released by being turned into the subject matter of the poem. Hence the exhortation to the self at beginning and end to keep on thinking, the only action which can neutralise the dangerously destructive mental condition engendered by the experience described. The poem thus is an implied comment on the power of art as well as an evocation of a powerful emotional theme.

4
KAIΣAPIΩN
Kaisarion

Εν μέρει γιά να εξακριβώσω μιά εποχή,
εν μέρει και την ώρα να περάσω,
την νύχτα χθές πήρα μιά συλλογή
επιγραφών των Πτολεμαίων να διαβάσω.
Οι άφθονοι έπαινοι κ' η κολακείες
εις όλους μοιάζουν. Όλοι είναι λαμπροί,
ένδοξοι, κραταιοί, άγαθοεργοί·
καθ' επιχείρησις των σοφοτάτη.
Αν πείς γιά τες γυναίκες της γενιάς, κι αυτές.
όλες η Βερενίκες, κ' η Κλεοπάτρες θαυμαστές.

Όταν κατόρθωσα την εποχή να εξακριβώσω
θάφινα το βιβλίο αν μιά μνεία μικρή.
κι ασήμαντη, του βασιλέως Καισαρίωνος
δεν είλκυε την προσοχή μου αμέσως ...

Α, να, ήρθες συ με την αόριστη
γοητεία σου. Στην ιστορία λίγες
γραμμές μονάχα βρίσκονται γιά σένα,
κ' έτσι πιό ελεύθερα σ' έπλασα μες στον νου μου.
Σ' έπλασα ωραίο κ' αισθηματικό.
Η τέχνη μου στο πρόσωπό σου δίνει
μιάν ονειρώδη συμπαθητική εμορφιά.
Και τόσο πλήρως σε φαντάσθηκα,
πού χθές την νύχτα αργά, σαν έσβυνεν
η λάμπα μου — άφισα επίτηδες να σβύνει —
εθάρεψα πού μπήκες μες στην κάμαρά μου,
με φάνηκε πού εμπρός μου στάθηκες· ως θα ήσουν
μες στην κατακτημένην Αλεξάνδρεια,
χλωμός και κουρασμένος, ιδεώδης εν τη λύπη σου,

81

C. P. Cavafy

ελπίζοντας ακόμη να σε σπλαχνισθούν
οι φαύλοι — πού ψιθύριζαν το << Πολυκαισαρίη >>.

This poem is unique in Cavafy's work for its combination of the themes of time, art and sensuality. The narrative line presents a simple incident. The poet, in checking up on some historical detail, comes across a reference to Caesarion, supposedly the son of Cleopatra by Julius Caesar, who was put to death by Octavian in 30 B.C. as part of his policy of removing potential rivals. The reference then sets off a melancholy but sensual reverie in which the boy is evoked in the stylised terms with which Cavafy customarily portrays beautiful youths. At first sight there is nothing exceptional about a narrative of this kind. But a dry synopsis of this kind gives remarkably little sense of what the poem actually conveys.

The poem is divided into three unequal stanzas. Its structure is essentially dramatic. In the first stanza, the poet is leafing through a collection of Ptolemaic inscriptions. In the second he comes across the reference to Caesarion. In the third he has his private vision of the boy. The progression of this structure is marked by the way the poet uses rhyme. Throughout the first section, while the speaker is recording the conventionality of the portrayal of the Ptolemies that he finds in the inscriptions, rhyme is plentiful, coming to a jaunty climax on the couplet in lines 9 and 10: ABABCAADEE. The four lines of the second section appear to be about to continue the rhyme-scheme of the previous stanza, but as the speaker finds the reference to Caesarion, the rhyme fades out and disappears for the rest of the poem. So rhyme here acts as a symbol of convention, disappearing from the poet's imagination as the figure of Caesarion takes hold of it.

If rhyme helps to shape the overall dramatic progress of the poem register differences, repetition, enjambement and musical patterning help to emphasise individual points in the development. In lines 5-10, as the speaker notes the sameness and the excessiveness of the language used about the Ptolemies, some of his own language itself becomes more stilted, not just in the adjectives taken from the inscriptions: καθ' ἐπιχείρησις τῶν σοφοτάτη. When Caesarion is first mentioned, the same formality of language—του βασιλέως Καισαρίωνος, εἵλκυε— links him to the other Ptolemies. And in the dream section, he becomes double: half evoked in a spoken style, Σ' ἔπλασα ὡραίο κ' αἰσθημα- τικό, half formal, ιδεώδης ἐν τῃ λύπῃ σου. The mingling of past and present time is marked by the two sorts of style.

But if Caesarion remains at least partly linked with the other Ptolemies in this way, in others he is deliberately separated from them. The monotonous uniformity of the picture of the Ptolemies which the speaker derives from his reading is strengthened by the repetitions of 'all' in emphatic positions: εις ὅλους at the beginning of line 6 before the verb which it qualifies, ὅλοι after the caesura in the same line, ὅλες at the beginning of line 10. This helps to create the sense of Caesarion as an exception, an exception created largely by history's failure to notice the boy. Furthering this point, Cavafy uses musical patterning to pick out the phrase μιά μνεία μικρή/κι ασήμαντη (ll.12-13), and enjambement to stress the words κι ασήμαντη and λίγες (1.16). Ασήμαντη is particularly important because it is ironic: what is insignificant to history is what becomes of great significance to the speaker. The adjective αόριστη on an enjambement at line 15 makes the point more precisely still. The word here means not so much 'undefinable' as 'undefined': Caesarion's charm lies in the fact that he is almost untouched by history and therefore leaves almost everything to the imagination.

It is natural, then, that what the poem emphasises next is the importance of imagination. This is achieved by the repetition of σ' ἔπλασα in ll.18-19, rephrased in the reference to η τέχνη μου in the following line and picked up again in σε φαντάσθηκα in 1.22. The Caesarion who will be evoked in the following lines never loses his historical ties, but he is at the same time, emphatically, the speaker's own creation, Caesarion as he would have liked to possess him. This power of the imagination to overthrow the limits of reality is similar in kind to that described in 'Το διπλανό τραπέζι', where the speaker 'remembers' sexually possessing a boy who, it is clear from the context, he can never have had. But in this case the process is not accidental but conscious: the vocabulary is that of the artist: 'I moulded you', 'My art gave you…'.

At this point, the element of sensuality is brought in to the poem very discreetly. The boy has the standard characteristics of Cavafy's youths, expressed in the usual stylised fashion: beauty (ωραίο), sensitivity (αισθηματικό), the ideal (ονειρώδη, ιδεώδης). The vision of the boy is itself a double process: first the imaginative projection created around the historical reference (ll. 19-21), then the further projection into an almost physical presence (ll. 22-30). This second vision is significantly placed μες στην κάμαρά μου (rooms in Cavafy are usually the scene of erotic encounters, as in 'Απ' τες εννιά' and 'Ο ήλιος του απογεύματος'), in a darkness wilfully encouraged by the speaker. But what is interesting about the vision is that the sensual side is not what is uppermost in the speaker's imagination. What emerges from the picture of pallor, weariness, grief and the desire for mercy which dominates the final three lines of the poem is the picture of the boy as victim, rather than the boy as lover. Cavafy brings out this theme of the victim in the musical parallel between the boy and Alexandria: the city is κατακτημένην, the boy κουρασμένος. Though the theme of the youth as victim may seem at first sight specific to this historical context, it does not really separate Caesarion from other Cavafy youths. For when one reflects on it, most of Cavafy's young men are losers: they lose their place in society, they lose their lovers, they lose their lives. The only winner is always the artist who recuperates them from time. Caesarion is no exception.

In 'Caesarion', then, fact and imagination meet in the personality and activity of the artist. But there is more to it than that, for 'fact' is itself a compound of two quite distinct forms of time: recorded, historical time, which is 'closed', unchanging, and everyday personal time, which is 'open-ended', ephemeral. The first four lines introduce these two sorts of time arranged in the pattern ABAABA:

να εξακριβώσω = personal time

μια εποχή = historical time

την ώρα να περάσω = personal time

την νύχτα χθες πήρα = personal time

μια συλλογή επιγραφών των Πτολεμαίων = historical time

να διαβάσω = personal time

Thus the two sorts of time are closely interwoven from the very beginning. This relationship is then reflected in a very complex relationship between time and verb tenses. Any poem in which a first person voice speaks is by definition a poem in the present. But the 'I' voice of this poem describes personal time in the past throughout: πήρα, κατόρθωσα, έπλασα, φαντάσθηκα, άφισα, εθάρεψα, με φάνηκε. Historical time, on the contrary, is in the present tense: μοιάζουν (1.6), είναι (1.6), βρίσκονται (1.17). The exception to this rule is Caesarion, who shares the speaker's past tenses—ήρθες (15), μπήκες (25), and who brings with him a historical moment in the past, the whispering voices of those who advised Octavian to have him killed. And just once, in the lines

Η τέχνη μου στο πρόσωπό σου δίνει

μιαν ονειρώδη συμπαθητική εμορφιά

the speaker himself moves into the present. This distribution of tenses is not accidental. Historical time is the eternal present: personal time is a succession of actions which pass and are lost. Caesarion is as much part of the speaker's personal time as of history, so he shares his role in the tense system of the poem. But art is both part of personal time and aspires to the permanence of historical time. It links the speaker and Caesarion, and it therefore partakes of both tense sequences: art as past action (σ' έπλασα) and as the permanent result (Η τέχνη μου στο πρόσωπό σου δίνει ...). I have carefully referred to the 'I' voice of the poem as 'the speaker'. But in fact 1.20 links the speaker's imagination to the poem in which it is recorded. Its present tense is the present of the poem itself.

When we look closely at 'Caesarion' in this way, we find that its form both dramatises its content and creates part of it. The poem illustrates the process of imaginative creation while discussing it. For the artist, the divisions of time disappear. The personal past and the historical present become one in the eternal present of the imagination. And whereas the eternal present of history tends to eliminate individuality:

Οι ἄφθονοι ἔπαινοι κ' η κολακείες
εις ὁλους μοιάζουν

the imagination recreates that individuality, even if in a stylised form. In this respect this poem is virtually a key to our whole understanding of Cavafy's work.

5
ΕΝ ΣΠΑΡΤΗ
In Sparta

Δεν ήξερεν ο βασιλεύς Κλεομένης, δεν τολμούσε —
δεν ήξερε έναν τέτοιον λόγο πώς να πεί
προς την μητέρα του: ότι απαιτούσε ο Πτολεμαίος
γιά εγγύησιν της συμφωνίας των ν' αποσταλεί κι αυτή
εις Αίγυπτον και να φυλάττεται·
λίαν ταπεινωτικόν, ανοίκειον πράγμα.
Κι όλο ήρχονταν γιά να μιλήσει· κι όλο δίσταζε.
Κι όλο άρχιζε να λέγει· κι όλο σταματούσε.

Μα η υπέροχη γυναίκα τον κατάλαβε
(είχεν ακούσει κιόλα κάτι διαδόσεις σχετικές),
και τον ενθάρρυνε να εξηγηθεί.
Και γέλασε· κ' είπε βεβαίως πιαίνει.
Και μάλιστα χαίρονταν πού μπορούσε ν'άναι
στο γήρας της οφέλιμη στην Σπάρτη ακόμη.

Όσο γιά την ταπείνωσι — μα αδιαφορούσε.
Το φρόνημα της Σπάρτης ασφαλώς δεν ήταν ικανός
να νοιώσει ένας Λαγίδης χθεσινός·
όθεν κ' η απαίτησίς του δεν μπορούσε
πραγματικώς να ταπεινώσει Δέσποιναν
Επιφανή ως αυτήν· Σπαρτιάτου βασιλέως μητέρα.

This poem dramatises a moment of late Spartan history, the request by
Ptolemy III that Kratisicleia, mother of the Spartan king Cleomenes,
should go to Egypt as a hostage, in guarantee of the Spartan-Egyptian
alliance against the Macedonian League. The poem thus handles a theme
developed in a comparable way in ''Άγε, ω βασιλεύ Λακεδαιμονίων'.
At the back of our minds we should hold onto the fact that Kratisicleia

was in fact murdered by Ptolemy IV as a result of this arrangement. Typically, Cavafy has chosen an event symbolic of the decline of past glories. The Spartans represent the Greek tradition at its most uncompromising. The humiliation represented by Ptolemy's demand, let alone by its bloody sequel, stands in implicit contrast to the glorious associations of Sparta at its height. Yet in the attitude of the Spartan queen the spirit of bravery and determination, the confidence in Greek values, the indifference to what Fate may bring are qualities which outlast the mere fact of political decline. They represent the sort of special quality difficult for an outsider to appreciate, just as Ptolemy, 'an upstart member of the Lagidae', is incapable of appreciating το φρόνημα της Σπάρτης.

The poem cannot, however, be taken as principally an approving account of Spartan virtue. The balance of elements within it indicates something more ironic than that. The two six-line stanzas which express the attitudes of the queen are prefixed by eight lines devoted to portraying the weakness and indecision of Cleomenes. Spartan virtue now resides, it would seem, in its women-folk rather than its warriors. This contrast is strongly brought out in the manner of the poem, which, despite its psychological flavour, is not descriptive, or even narrative, so much as dramatic. There is a notable absence of visual detail. The few adjectives are evaluative, i.e. they tell us about a character's values, not about physical qualities: 6 ταπεινωτικόν, ανοίκειον, 9 υπέροχη, 14 οφέλιμη, 16 ικανός. We are not looking at events from outside, but responding to them through two different minds. The poem places side by side the inner feelings of the two characters and allows them to form an implicit commentary upon one another.

How is this dramatic effect created? In the first five lines, the climax is Ptolemy's outrageous demand. But it takes us a long time to get there. The syntax constantly restarts: there are three switches of vocabulary, from ήξερεν to τολμούσε and back to ήξερε, before we appear to reach the essential point of the sentence. And in fact that essential point is delayed yet again by the opaque phrase έναν τέτοιον λόγο, made more disturbing by the stress which the unnatural word order places on it. Plainly something is troubling the king, but what? The use of three enjambements adds to the suspense. The first (2-3) emphasises προς την μητέρα του, the second (3-4) emphasises Ptolemy and delays the nature of his demand; the third emphasises κι αυτή. Cavafy carefully arranges both the form and the content of the whole five lines so that the tension is maintained to the last. Why is Cleomenes so palpably nervous and hesitant? What has he got to say to his mother that is so difficult to come out with? What can Ptolemy be demanding 'as a guarantee of their agreement'? The climax is thus the very last phrase of this long first sentence: και να φυλάττεται. The queen is to be no more and no less than a hostage. Cleomenes' state of mind and the problem facing him are thus unfolded to the reader in such a way that the dramatic nature of the situation is actualised in its expression. The evaluation of the situation:

λίαν ταπεινωτικόν, ανοίκειον πράγμα

is then given in a single line, grammatically detached by the punctuation. This makes it possible to read it not just as an evaluation of the situation itself by the king, but also as a psychological comment on both the king's acceptance of Ptolemy's terms and his indecision in the face of the need to communicate them to his mother. As such, the evaluation leads naturally back into the restatement of the theme of indecision in lines 7–8.

This is a stylistic 'return' too. Here again is the mirroring of actions in word patterns with which the poem began—the repetition of κι όλο, the rephrasing of the first clause of 7 in the first clause of 8, the cumulative sense of unfinished action created by the series of imperfect tenses. The circularity of movement in the stanza is aided by the musical pattern of the words at line-end: though there is no rhyme as such, we are aware of the matching of σταματούσε in 8 to τολμούσε in 1 because Cavafy makes a definite pattern out of end-words stressed on the penultimate, final and antepenultimate syllables: ABABCACA.

Rhythmically, as well as thematically, the stanza ends up where it began. In fact, put crudely, it is a virtuoso embodiment of vacillation. It therefore stands in complete contrast to the decisiveness of what follows. In the second stanza the queen's calmness of voice can be detected in the style of the reported speech-cum-narrative just as Cleomenes' indecision is mirrored in the opening words. There is only one enjambement in the second stanza, and that serves to emphasise 'in her old age' at the beginning of line 14. There are verbs in the simple past tense, indicating completed action. There are no repetitions. Just as behind l.2 we 'hear' Cleomenes say 'I don't know how to tell her...', so in l.10 we hear Kratisicleia's off-hand 'I have already heard rumours...'. This impression of two contrasted voices is encouraged by a shift in the two stanzas between a slightly more formal level of language in the first, with a classicising ring about it that emphasises the king's awareness of his own status (προς την μητέρα, λίαν ταπεινωτικόν, ανοίκειον πράγμα), and, in the second, the consciously relaxed syntax of the phrase είπε βεβαίως πιαίνει, and the insertion of conversational μάλιστα and the contraction ν'άναι in l.13.

The difference between the two characters which emerges immediately in stanzas 1 and 2 then becomes the basis for an elaborate stylistic irony in stanza 3. For Cavafy now uses a number of elements associated in stanza 1 with Cleomenes—imperfect tenses, enjambements and linguistic formality—to stress the presence in Kratisicleia, of all the qualities absent in the king. The illusion of a colloquial voice is maintained—the placing of μα to break the direction of the syntax in l.15, the adverbs ασφαλώς and πραγματικώς (formal forms but used conversationally) the relatively colloquial adjective χθεσινός. But the language has a great deal of formality, notably το φρόνημα, η απαίτησις, and the morphology and word order of Σπαρτιάτου βασιλέως μητέρα. (Perhaps it should noted at this point that Kratiscleia is at no point given her name or even the title of queen: what counts is her *role* as mother to the royal line.) The imperfect tenses here suggest no hesitation, they show firmly entrenched beliefs—'she didn't care', 'it wasn't possible'. The enjambements do not withhold an unpalatable fact: they build up to a positive climax: they emphasise the incapacity of Ptolemy, the impossibility of his humbling a Spartan queen, they culminate in Επιφανή ως αυτήν, emphasising both the adjective, by dividing it from its noun across line-end, and the phrase ως αυτήν, which recalls Cleomenes' nervous κι αυτής in l.4.

To the king, his mother's status is an embarrassment in this humiliating political arrangement. To her, her status is inviolate and cannot be touched by a mere Ptolemy. The patterning is even more elaborate than this summary suggests. In ll.1-3 enjambement leads to a phrase τέτοιον λόγο which is then redefined by a clause in apposition—Ptolemy and his ignominious demands. In ll.18-20 enjambement also leads to a phrase, επιφανή ως αυτήν, which is then redefined by a phrase in apposition, but this time the line ends not on Ptolemy but on the 'mother of a Spartan King'. The tone is not apologetic but triumphant. Cavafy is not concerned in all this to discuss the rights and wrongs of the situation. He creates a dramatic opposition between indecision and weakness in the king and supreme confidence in the queen. One could very well apply to this sort of poetic construction the term which the English poet Robert Browning used for some of his own poetry: dramatic lyrics. The attention to rhythmic effects, the careful placing of words or phrases, the matching of formal and informal language, the use of stylistic irony to reflect thematic contrast, are techniques of lyric poetry. But the emphasis on action and characterisation, the sense of contrasting voices, are primarily dramatic devices. Out of the tension of these elements grows the reader's awareness of the ambiguities of the historical event and its participants, but this awareness is almost ancillary to the aesthetic pleasure which the careful matching of content to form produces.

6
Η ΜΑΧΗ ΤΗΣ ΜΑΓΝΗΣΙΑΣ
The Battle of Magnesia

Έχασε την παληά του ορμή, το θάρρος του.
Του κουρασμένου σώματός του, του άρρωστου

σχεδόν, θάχει κυρίως την φροντίδα. Κι ο επίλοιπος
βίος του θα διέλθει αμέριμνος. Αυτά ο Φίλιππος

τουλάχιστον διατείνεται. Απόψι κύβους παίζει·
έχει όρεξι να διασκεδάσει. Στο τραπέζι

βάλτε πολλά τριαντάφυλλα. Τι αν στην Μαγνησία
ο Αντίοχος κατεστράφηκε. Λένε πανωλεθρία

έπεσ' επάνω στού λαμπρού στρατεύματος τα πλήθια.
Μπορεί να τα μεγάλωσαν· όλα δεν θάναι αλήθεια.

Είθε. Γιατί αγκαλά κ' εχθρός, ήσανε μιά φυλή.
Όμως ένα <<είθε>> είν' αρκετό. Ίσως κιόλας πολύ.

Ο Φίλιππος την εορτή βέβαια δεν θ' αναβάλει.
Όσο κι αν στάθηκε του βίου του η κόπωσις μεγάλη,

ένα καλό διατήρησεν η μνήμη διόλου δεν του λείπει.
Θυμάται πόσο στην Συρία θρήνησαν, τι είδος λύπη

είχαν, σαν έγινε σκουπίδι η μάνα των Μακεδονία. —
Ν' αρχίσει το τραπέζι. Δούλοι· τους αυλούς, τη φωταψία.

The title of this poem indicates that Cavafy requires his readers to know the nature and significance of the Battle of Magnesia. At this battle, which took place in 190 B.C., the Romans defeated Antiochus the Third of Syria, one of the Greek-speaking kingdoms which resulted from the splintering of Alexander the Great's empire, confiscated a portion of his territories and thus secured a permanent presence in the Greek East. This identifies the Philip of the poem as Philip the Fifth of Macedon, who had himself recently been defeated by the Romans at the battle of Cynoscephalae (197 B.C.), where Antiochus failed to assist him.

This is a disconcerting poem, because nothing about it is quite what it seems. Thematically it appears to be a study in a particular historical moment, showing how personal considerations outweigh political ones, and thereby emphasising the permanently fragmented nature of the Greek world. But all sorts of details in the structure, rhythm, narrative manner and choice of language undermine so didactic a reading. They need to be explored before we can read the poem properly.

Ostensibly it is a poem which tells a story. But the rapidly changing person and tense of the verb are disconcerting: ll.1-2 are in the past tense, 3-4 in the future, 5-6 in the present. In 1-4 we have an unidentified 3rd person singular, who becomes 'Philip' at the end of line 4; but in line 7 a 2nd person plural imperative appears. Cavafy is in fact introducing a technique we have seen him favour in other historical poems, his own version of 'free indirect speech', the indirect representation of what a character is thinking. Philip is present as both an objective entity, seen from the outside, and a subjective one, seen from the inside. The language moves in an out of descriptive (external) and psychological (internal) perspectives by shifting person and tense. To stress the inner voice, as well as the imperatives there are grammatical constructions which imply speech/thought—τι αν ... , είθε, the ellipse of verbs in 11-12. Similarly, certain adverbs are used to mark thought processes, βέβαια for example; in particular, όμως and κιόλας are markers of Philip's hesitation. On the other hand, τουλάχιστον (l.5, emphasised by the enjambement across the couplet) suggests an outside judgement, and strengthens the idea of the difference between what Philip proclaims and some deeper reality.

The structure of the poem is no easier to determine that its genre. Though it appears to be a simple set of nine couplets, it in fact falls into two parts which are marked in a unexpected way. First, by enjambement. At the beginning, the enjambement is so thick as to distort the rhythm/rhyme pattern: new rhythmic shapes grow up not only across lines but across couplets. There are enjambements between 2-3, 3-4, 4-5, 5-6, 6-7, 7-8, 8-9. But there is not another until 16-17. The second dividing factor is the rhyme. All the rhymes are rich except three, notably stanzas 4 and 9 (lines 7-8 and 17-18). These two couplets are also the only ones in which two words in the same gender, number and grammatical category are rhymed. And they also contain the two geographical references which represent the Greek kingdoms at question in the poem: Magnesia (in Lydia) where Antiochus has just been defeated, and Macedonia, Philip's kingdom, and, through the connection with Alexander, mother to all the extant Greek kingdoms of the period, including Syria. If we match the division by enjambement against the division by type of rhyme, we find that the poem pivots around the central couplet, 9-10. In other words, it pivots around Philip's reaction to the news of Antiochus' defeat.

What picture of Philip's reaction to that news does the poem in fact project? It starts apparently factually, ('he lost', 'he will care for'). We have no identification of who 'he' is at this point. Only retrospectively does it become plain that this is an inner voice, formulating a decision to take life easy. But this decision is, as the phrase αυτά ... διατείνεται emphasises, an assertion rather than a reality, and one which the emphatic 'at least' (1.5) undermines. The character in focus is Philip of Macedon, and the intrusive narrator has cast doubt on the reality of his view of present and future. At one level, after his defeat by the Romans he has no real choice but to accept political detachment. But the claim that his life will be 'carefree' (1.4) is more open to question. What is dramatic about Cavafy's presentation here is that the reader senses the mood before he knows the reason for it. Only the title might give us any clue.

Η ΜΑΧΗ ΤΗΣ ΜΑΓΝΗΣΙΑΣ

This is where the enjambements play their part. The words in ll.1-8 may assert detachment and a desire for self-preservation, but the rhythm is nervous and irregular, breaking down the ostensible serene regularity of the rhyming couplet form, and creating a predominance of short grammatical units. Even when the opening insists on diversion (ll.5-7), the reality of the carefree existence is thrown into doubt, since the simple references to dice and an appetite for entertainment can equally be read as indicators of Philip's determination to be detached rather than as a description of his achievement of detachment.

This sense of ambiguity is reinforced by the fact that the references to entertainment are followed by a section of reflections which at last explain the nervous tenor of the opening rhythms. The whole of the central section (7b-12) records a constantly changing mental review of the political situation: τι αν, μπορεί να, δεν θα, αγκαλά, όμως, ίσως. The rumoured outcome of the battle of Magnesia causes Philip perceptible agitation; his decision to ignore it is a process of self-persuasion. The only two extended grammatical units in the poem represent, respectively, the consideration of the destruction of Antiochus' troops (9-10) and Philip's memory of how the Syrians reacted to his own defeat (16-17). This rhythmic similarity pairs the two sets of reflexions with the help of the Magnesia/Macedonia rhyme pattern already noted.

Each of the two units also has its own stylistic development. In the first unit, the report of the destruction of Antiochus' forces is couched in high-sounding, very musical language. It is the first time in the poem that a single grammatical unit has filled a whole line; it contains the term πανωλεθρία and the 'poetic' inversion στου λαμπρού στρατεύματος τα πλήθια, and it is notable for its patterns of p and l sounds and the striking extended pattern

Λένε πανωλεθρία
έπεσ' επάνω (...)

This is in marked contrast with the second line of the couplet, which is

95

in a purely colloquial, prosaic demotic, and contains Philip's rejection of the rumours. The second unit (16-17) marks the moment when Philip finally masters his agitation. It comes at the end of a series of ironic musical connections, koposis/ kalo, mnimi/ thrinisan/ lipi, the two groups being united in skoupidi, which creates a sense of highly controlled language. It is as though Philip's concentration on his own sense of injury helps, paradoxically, to calm him. So that when the short grammatical units and fragmented rhythm return in the last line, with the return of the theme of merry-making, they seem decisive, rather than nervous.

What the poem contains then is a technically very sophisticated study in the reflection of the changing moods of an historical character at a moment at which the pressures of personal and political interests and emotions are brought to bear upon him. By showing us Philip from the inside and the outside concurrently, with the complex shifts of voice and person which that entails, Cavafy suggests the ambiguous relationship between the public persona (the carefree reveller) and the private one (nervous reflection on the events and their significance). But the poem remains a psychological and aesthetic study.

A footnote: Cavafy was reproached by the botanist Sareyannis for his reference to roses at Philip's feast. Sareyannis claimed that this must be historically inaccurate, since it would be the wrong season, the battle of Magnesia having taken place in December. Cavafy defended his reference on historical grounds—the winter export of roses from Egypt to Italy is attested, Philip was a rich king. But poetically the historical accuracy is neither here nor there. The associations of the rose in the European tradition with passing pleasures ('gather ye rosebuds'—also in Greek poetry after Christopoulos) are entirely appropriate to Philip's move, and the word is musically connected to βάλτε and τραπέζι.

7

ΦΙΛΕΛΛΗΝ
Philhellene

Την χάραξι φρόντισε τεχνικά να γίνει.
Έκφρασις σοβαρή και μεγαλοπρεπής.
Το διάδημα καλλίτερα μάλλον στενό·
εκείνα τα φαρδιά τών Πάρθων δεν με αρέσουν.
Η επιγραφή, ως σύνηθες, ελληνικά·
όχ' υπερβολική, όχι πομπώδης —
μην τα παρεξηγήσει ο ανθύπατος
πού όλο σκαλίζει και μηνά στην Ρώμη —
αλλ' όμως βέβαια τιμητική.
Κάτι πολύ εκλεκτό απ' το άλλο μέρος·
κανένας δισκοβόλος έφηβος ωραίος.
Προ πάντων σε συστείνω να κυττάξεις
(Σιθάσπη, προς θεού, να μη λησμονηθεί)
μετά το Βασιλεύς και το Σωτήρ,
να χαραχθεί με γράμματα κομψά, Φιλέλλην.
Και τώρα μη με αρχιζεις ευφυολογίες,
τα <<Πού οι Έλληνες; >> και <<Πού τα Ελληνικά
πίσω απ' τον Ζάγρο εδώ, απο τα Φράατα πέρα>>.
Τόσοι και τόσοι βαρβαρότεροι μας άλλοι
αφού το γράφουν, θα το γράψουμε κ' εμείς.
Και τέλος μη ξεχνάς που ενίοτε
μας έρχοντ' από την Συρία σοφισταί,
και στιχοπλόκοι, κι άλλοι ματαιόσπουδοι.
Ώστε ανελλήνιστοι δεν είμεθα, θαρρώ.

This poem is another dramatic monologue after the manner of Robert
Browning. There are two implied characters, one addressing the other,
who remains silent, though his reactions are implied. The speaker is
evidently a minor Eastern ruler: 'out here beyond Zagro, further than

Phraata' points to somewhere east of Parthia, deep into the lands of the former Persian Empire. The princeling is giving instructions to a courtier called Sithaspis on the the engraving of a coin or perhaps a medallion.

The poem is often interpreted as putting down the pretensions of those on the fringes of Hellenism. Yet the inscription engraved on the coin is not to read 'Hellene' but 'Philhellene'. It is perhaps worth making a comparison with other poems by Cavafy in which non-Greek characters with pretensions to Greek culture are portrayed. In 'Ηγεμών εκ Δυτικής Λιβύης' a foreigner who wishes to pass for a Greek but is barely able to speak Greek is presented in a comical light, although the joke is partly on those who take him for a profound thinker merely because he says very little. Cavafy's attitude here is similar to that in one of the so-called unpublished poems, 'Επάνοδος', where what he criticises in the oriental princelings is their fear of revealing their own Eastern-ness. In 'Philhellene' he is less concerned with what is being hidden than what is being displayed. The speaker does not even reject the broad diadem because it is Parthian, but because he does not like it. The theme of the poem is much closer in this respect to that of another unpublished poem, 'Νομίσματα', where Cavafy seems rather touched by the Greek names attached to Eastern faces on oriental coins. What the reader has to evaluate is the character of the speaker as revealed by his monologue. And in fact the character of the speaker is more ambiguous than a purely negative reading allows for.

To see how this ambiguity is created, let us start by looking at the thematic structure of the monologue. It falls into three sections. Lines 1-11 are taken up with instructions about the image on the coin (2-4), the inscription (5-9), and the picture to go on the obverse (10-11). In lines 12-15 the speaker returns to the subject of the inscription in more detail, his words coming to a climax on 'Philhellene'. Line 16 implies reaction on the part of the courtier addressed, generating, in 16-24, the princeling's defence of his 'Greekness'.

Certain formal features help to punctuate this structure. In the first section no grammatical units overrun line ends. Indeed, in lines 1-5 and

10-11 sense, grammar and line all finish together. The lines are rather telegraphic: 2-3 and 5-11 have no main verb; in fact 2-3, 5-6, 9-11 have no verbs at all. The effect is rather brisk. The speaker appears to be a man who does not waste words. But when he returns to the subject of the inscription in the second section, his manner is rather different. The four lines of this section are made up of a single sentence with a marked rhythmic effect at the end. Line 14 is one of three lines in the poem which have only 10 syllables; line 15 has thirteen. This would not automatically have any particular musical effect. But because of its grammatical structure, line 15 breaks into two groups, 10 syllables + 3. The ear thus hears two rhythmically similar ten syllable lines and a separate three syllable unit:

μετά το Βασιλεύς και το Σωτήρ
να χαραχθεί με γράμματα κομψά,
Φιλέλλην

In other words, the key word of the section, Φιλέλλην, is isolated in relation to the rhythm of the previous line, and this isolation gives it great stress. The implied reaction of Sithaspis at the beginning of the next section causes a change in the rhythm of the monologue. For the first time we have constructions which run over line-end (17-18, 19-20, 21-22). Only the last line returns to the emphatic sense = sentence = line structure of the first section. Significantly, in these more turbulent lines the speaker is on the defensive, as he tries to justify his claim to Greekness. In other words, complexity of syntax and metre really start in 12-15, when the subject of the inscription 'Philhellene' is raised. And it is on the subject of language alone that the speaker loses his cool: the only enjambements come when he is making the point that 'there are greater barbarians than we are' and that 'we get our share of Greek culture'.

Within this carefully structured narrative the speaker both wears a mask and ironises that mask. He has pretensions, but he makes fun of them himself. Τόσοι και τόσοι βαρβαρότεροι μας άλλοι (l.19), in its implicit acknowledgement that he himself is a 'barbarian', shows an awareness that the adoption of outward Greek trimmings, particularly language, is only superficial. Yet his aesthetic sensibilities, if nothing else, justify his sense of affinity to Greek culture. Note the evidence of sensitivity to art both in details of vocabulary (ll.1 τεχνικά, 10 εκλεκτό, 15 κομψά) and in the stress given to χάραξι, τεχνικά and ωραίος by word order. Note also his sensitivity to male beauty (l.11), and to the idea of 'nothing in excess' (1.6).

As well as aesthetic sensibility, he displays a sense of humour. The form of words in which he forestalls Sithaspis' objections (ll.16-18) is rather comic. And above all he has some sense of critical perspective: the choice of the words στιχοπλόκοι and ματαιόσπουδοι shows that he has no illusions about the quality of Greek cultural ambassador that penetrates beyond the Euphrates, and even these words are modified by the emphasis on 'sometimes' at the enjambement in line 21. This oriental princeling does have some of the accomplishments and standards of a Hellene. On the other hand there are disturbingly absurd features in the monologue too: in lines 2-4, the obsession with the physical image; in 7-8 the concern with the political image; in 9 the insistence on the honorific element. The man is, perhaps, over-aware of his own status. So that at one level we have the impression of a slightly ridiculous self-important figure.

Does the poem allow us to be sure what is mask and what is naive reality? The key question is: what stylistic weight are we to give the consciously katharevousa linguistic forms (ανελλήνιστοι and είμεθα) in the last line? The answer must surely be that they potentially function both ironically and seriously, and that their irony is partly intended by the speaker, partly directed against him. They stand in contrast with the colloquial style of the monologue as a whole, and reflect the language of the sophists and rhymesters the prince himself has just referred to so slightingly. They represent the weakness in his cultural armoury. His claims to the title of Philhellene are least justified in the area of language, yet that is the area which most obsesses him.

8
ΜΥΡΗΣ· ΑΛΕΞΑΝΔΡΕΙΑ ΤΟΥ 340 Μ.Χ.
Myres: Alexandria 340 A.D.

Την συμφορά όταν έμαθα, πού ο Μύρης πέθανε,
πήγα στο σπίτι του, μ' όλο πού το αποφεύγω
να εισέρχομαι στων Χριστιανών τα σπίτια,
προ πάντων όταν έχουν θλίψεις η γιορτές.

Στάθηκα σε διάδρομο. Δεν θέλησα
να προχωρήσω πιό εντός, γιατί αντελήφθην
πού οι συγγενείς του πεθαμένου μ' έβλεπαν
με προφανή απορίαν και με δυσαρέσκεια.

Τον είχανε σε μιά μεγάλη κάμαρη
πού από την άκρην όπου στάθηκα
είδα κομάτι· όλο τάπητες πολύτιμοι,
και σκεύη εξ αργύρου και χρυσού.

Στέκομουν κ' έκλαια σε μία άκρη του διαδρόμου.
Και σκέπτομουν πού η συγκεντρώσεις μας κ' η εκδρομές
χωρίς τον Μύρη δεν θ' αξίζουν πιά
και σκέπτομουν πού πια δέ θα τον δω
στα ωραία κι άσεμνα ξενύχτια μας
να χαίρεται, και να γελά, και ν' απαγγέλλει στίχους
με την τελεία του αίσθησι του ελληνικού ρυθμού·
και σκέπτομουν πού έχασα γιά πάντα
την εμορφιά του, πού έχασα γιά πάντα
τον νέον πού λάτρευα παράφορα.

Κάτι γρηές, κοντά μου, χαμηλά μιλούσαν γιά
την τελευταία μέρα πού έζησε —
στα χείλη του διαρκώς τ' όνομα του Χριστού,
στα χέρια του βαστούσ' έναν σταυρό. —

101

Μπήκαν κατόπι μες στην κάμαρη
τέσσαρες Χριστιανοί ιερείς, κ' έλεγαν προσευχές
ενθέρμως και δεήσεις στον Ιησούν,
η στήν Μαρίαν (δεν ξέρω την θρησκεία τους καλά).

Γνωρίζαμε, βεβαίως, πού ο Μύρης ήταν Χριστιανός.
Από την πρώτην ώρα το γνωρίζαμε, όταν
πρόπερσι στην παρέα μας είχε μπεί.
Μα ζούσεν απολύτως σαν κ' εμάς.
Απ' όλους μας πιό έκδοτος στες ηδονές·
σκορπώντας αφειδώς το χρήμα του στες διασκεδάσεις.
Γιά την υπόληψι του κόσμου ξένοιαστος,
ρίχνονταν πρόθυμα σε νύχτιες ρήξεις στές οδούς
όταν ετύχαινε η παρέα μας
να συναντήσει αντίθετη παρέα.
Ποτέ γιά την θρησκεία του δε μιλούσε.
Μάλιστα μιά φορά τον είπαμε
πώς θα τον πάρουμε μαζύ μας στο Σεράπιον.
Όμως σαν να δυσαρεστήθηκε
μ' αυτόν μας τον αστεϊσμό: θυμούμαι τώρα.
Α κι άλλες δυό φορές τώρα στον νου μου έρχονται.
Όταν στον Ποσειδώνα κάμναμε σπονδές.
τραβήχθηκε απ' τον κύκλο μας, κ' έστρεψε αλλού το βλέμμα.
Όταν ενθουσιασμένος ένας μας
είπεν, Η συντροφιά μας νάναι υπό
την εύνοιαν και την προστασίαν του μεγάλου,
του πανωραίου Απόλλωνος — ψιθύρισεν ο Μύρης
(οι άλλοι δεν άκουσαν) <<τη εξαιρέσει εμού>>.

Οι Χριστιανοί ιερείς μεγαλοφώνως
γιά την ψυχή του νέου δέονταν. —
Παρατηρούσα με πόση επιμέλεια,
και με τι προσοχήν εντατική
στούς τύπους της θρησκείας τους, ετοιμάζονταν
όλα γιά την χριστιανική κηδεία.
Κ' εξαίφνης με κυρίευσε μιά αλλόκοτη
εντύπωσις. Αόριστα, αισθάνομουν
σαν νάφευγεν από κοντά μου ο Μύρης·

ΜΥΡΗΣ· ΑΛΕΞΑΝΔΡΕΙΑ ΤΟΥ 340 Μ.Χ.

αισθάνομουν πού ενώθη, Χριστιανός,
με τους δικούς του, και πού γένομουν
ξ έ ν ο ς εγώ ξ έ ν ο ς π ο λ ύ· ένοιωθα κιόλα
μιά αμφιβολία να με σιμόνει· μήπως κ' είχα γελασθεί
από το πάθος μου, και π ά ν τ α τού ήμουν ξένος. —
Πετάχθηκα έξω απ' το φρικτό τους σπίτι,
έφυγα γρήγορα πριν αρπαχθεί, πριν αλλοιωθεί
απ' την χριστιανοσύνη τους η θύμηση του Μύρη.

The scene and characters of this poem are apparently imaginary. The period chosen, carefully indicated by the very precise date in the title, is one of civil and religious disturbance. Constantine the Great had died in 337. There was civil war in the West between two of his sons, with the eventual victory of Constans in 340. In the East the third son was occupied by a war with Persia. These were also the dying years of paganism, which was to flourish again only briefly, under the Emperor Julian. At the same time Christianity itself was a divided force. The struggle within the Alexandrian Christian community between the followers of Arius and those of Athanasius had started up again, since the death of Constantine had enabled Athanasius to return from his exile in Rome. The poem does not refer to any of this instability as such, but it explores the effects of a divided society. In that general sense the date 340 A.D. is suitably emblematic of the theme of division.

At the start of the poem we do not know that the speaker is Myres's lover. This only emerges at the end of the fourth section (ll.20-22). On the other hand, the fact that the speaker is not a Christian is established at the outset (ll.2-3). The first three verses (all quatrains) are in fact devoted to creating a sense that the speaker is entering an alien environment—his reluctance to go into a Christian house, especially at a time of mourning or rejoicing (ll.2-4), his hesitation once he is inside (ll.5-6), the hostility he detects in the attitude of the dead boy's relatives (7-8), even the richness of the environment in which the dead boy is being kept (9-12). There is continual emphasis, in the details of the scene, on what

103

divides the visitor from the Christian group. The speaker can only see *a bit* of the room from the *edge* where he is standing. And the use of the phrase τον είχανε (rather than a simple 'he was'), featured at the opening of the third stanza, puts the dead Myres very much in the possession of the relatives who show such displeasure at the sight of their unexpected visitor.

The tone of these opening stanzas is direct and conversational. The word order and vocabulary having nothing consciously poetic in them at all . Such effects of emphasis as there are come mostly from the frequent enjambements and the positioning of words in the line. Συμφορά and πέθανε are matched at either end of line 1 to establish the nature of the event from which the poem stems. The reluctance of the speaker to mix with Christians is underlined by the use of αποφεύγω and δεν θέλησα at line-end with enjambement. The placing of αντελήφθην and μ' έβλεπαν on adjacent line-ends (6-7) emphasises the division between the two groups, the speaker and Myres's relatives, which the second and third stanzas portray. The whole of the section forms a cinematic 'panning in' on the tableau of the corpse, the mourners, and the invisible barrier between them and the pagan friend. The tenses are narrative tenses describing a series of actions: 'I learnt', 'I went', 'I stood' (twice). The evident shift at the very beginning of stanza four to imperfects— στέκομουν, σκέπτομουν—then marks a clear change of thematic focus. We have entered the second section of the poem.

This second section is a single ten-line stanza. It starts by taking details from the previous narrative section and developing them. In l.5 we saw the speaker standing 'in a corridor'; in l.13 this is repeated in an expanded form, incorporating the image of standing 'at the edge' from l.10 and introducing a new element, that of emotional reaction (έκλαια). The time-sequence of the narrative is suspended, as we move from external action into the psychological time of internal reflection, empha- sised by the triple repetition of και σκέπτομουν in the same position in lines 14, 16 and 20. This opens a new phase in the poem—the exploration of the memory of the past—but as yet the speaker is more concerned with the implications for the present and future. His thoughts are focussed on the theme of loss, and the intensity of that sense of loss grows as the stanza progresses, the repetition of πιά (15-16) intensifying into the repetition of πού έχασα για πάντα (21-22). But these reflections also serve to 'place' the characters of both the speaker and Myres for us for the first time. Though a Christian and a pagan they were part of the same παρέα, a gang of young men given over to pleasure. The key lines are 17-19, with their three elements: άσεμνα ξενύχτια and its implications of sexual pleasure; χαίρεται and γελά showing light-hearted amusement; and the aesthetic sense revealed by the ability to recite Greek poetry well. At the climax of the section the relationship emerges as not just that of companions, but of lovers, Cavafy keeping the revealing phrase πού λάτρευα παράφορα for the very end of the stanza. To the physical separation which was the theme of the first three stanzas the poet has now added the theme of emotional separation. And, again, the language of the section has created its effects very simply: from enjambements, repetitions and the placing of words for dramatic effect.

The importance of the setting and events of the poem is now fully revealed. The speaker feels doubly unacceptable to Myres's family, because of his religion and his sexual inclinations. But we have not reached the climax. Instead, in the third section (ll.23-30), Cavafy turns our eyes, with the speaker's, back into the room, and records the details of what is happening there. The first part of the narrative (the old women's account of Myres's last hours) incorporates the dead boy into the Christianity of the scene for the first time. The link between boy and religion is neatly strengthened by musical patterning, firstly of st / h / i / and ou in 'on his lips' and 'of Christ':

στα χείλη του (...) Χριστού

then of st / h / r / and ou in 'of Christ' and 'in his hands':

Χριστού / στα χέρια του

and finally of sta / r / and v in 'held in his hands' and 'cross':

στα χέρια του βαστοῦσ' (...) σταυρό.

This harmonious picture of perfect piety clashes disconcertingly with the pagan sensualist remembered by the lover in ll.17-19. The subsequent arrival of the priests and the beginning of the service give an opportunity to emphasise the lover's confusion at, and exclusion from, what he is watching. It is very much an alien ritual—(...) δεν ξέρω την θρησκεία τους καλά (l.30). In this stanza then, the theme of otherness, of being on the edge of a hostile environment, which was carefully established in verses 1-12, is now repeated and intensified. For the first time, though the speaker does not formulate it, a division is hinted at not just between the lover and Myres's family and environment, but between the lover and Myres himself.

Just as the first and second sections of the poem move from external perspective to inner reflection, so do the third and fourth. The speaker has been watching the alien Christian ritual. It sets off a train of thought in which he himself begins to be aware of the Christianity of Myres as an element of otherness. Cavafy's technique here is an ironic one. We watch the speaker trying to persuade himself that this 'otherness' is illusory, that the real Myres is the one he knew and loved. The first two lines of the section emphasise the idea of knowledge (repetition of γνωρίζαμε)—yet it was a superficial and inadequate knowledge, because it never revealed the significance of Myres's Christianity. Instead of accepting this, the speaker begins by reassuring himself with a portrait of Myres as *similar* to himself. He dwells on the pleasure-loving role in the activities of the παρέα. The key words tend to come for emphasis at line end: 'like us' (34), 'pleasure' (35), 'entertainment' (36). The climax of this half of the stanza comes at l.41: Ποτέ για την θρησκεία του δε μιλούσε—note the emphatic word order. But this brings into the lover's memory three occasions—one known only to him—on which Myres's Christianity did briefly surface as a divisive factor. Notice the use of μάλιστα, θυμούμαι τώρα, and especially 'Α κι άλλες δυό φορές τώρα στον νου μου έρχονται (1.46), to emphasise the *process* of thought. The poem is a double drama: the drama of the events in Myres's house, and the drama of doubt which the speaker undergoes as a result of those events. More that that. All the events of the narrative are in the simple past or the imperfect. The present tenses in ll.45 and 46 (θυμούμαι, έρχονται) are strictly in a time sequence outside that of the action of the poem. They represent the time of retelling the events, and emphasise the lasting nature of the growth of doubt which the funeral scene engenders. This is important for our overall interpretation of the poem.

At the opening of the last stanza, we return once more to the scene in the house. Indeed, μεγαλοφώνως suggests the literal intrusion of physical reality into the lover's reflections. The emphasis on Christian priests and Christian funeral maintains the sense of otherness. But there is now no separation between narrative and psychological tenses. What happens outside the speaker is in the imperfect, and eventually what happens inside him includes simple past tenses. The moment has come where the physical and emotional aspects of the poem are completely interdependent. It is at 1.60 that the dramatic reaction finally occurs, marked by the placing of the adjective αλλόκοτη on the enjambement. The lover suddenly feels that he is losing Myres to the alien world around him. Notice how cause and effect are given a musical link in ll.58-60: χριστιανική, κηδεία, κυρίευσε and αλλόκοτη. As the conviction that the present is robbing him of the past grows, the relation between line and grammatical unit grows more disordered; the enjambements in ll.64-67 emphasise ξένος (which is then repeated), αμφιβολία and γελασθεί, leading to a third ξένος at line-end. Notice how, for the first time, Myres's name is at line-end every time it occurs in this section. The helplessness of the lover is reflected in the grammatical constructions in which he figures: he is the object (a doubt *approaches* him), or governs a verb in the passive (perhaps he *has been* deceived) or at least passive in form (αισθάνομουν twice, γένομουν). At 1.68 this helplessness resolves abruptly into violent action—πετάχθηκα, ἔφυγα γρήγορα— in order to prevent equally violent action being wrought upon him—πριν αρπαχθεί, πριν αλλοιωθεί. What he is seeking to preserve is the memory of Myres. He has already lost the present and the future: now he is afraid of losing the past, of losing something which is literally a part of himself.

It is the same panic-inspiring fear explored in a different way in 'Εν απογνώσει', with which I began this series of commentaries. But in 'Μύρης' there is an additional paradox which offers a final irony. As I said earlier, those present tenses in the fourth section (ll.45-46) reflect the way in which the doubt never *can* be finally expunged. Even after the event, as the speaker recasts it into the narrative of the poem, new evidence of Myres's otherness comes back to him. The Christians are winning there, just as they will win the religious battle against the pagans—e.g. by the destruction of the temple of Serapis (in 392 A.D.) where Myres had refused to accompany the παρέα. Hence we cannot accept Edmund Keeley's assessment that the ultimate act of faith for a pleasure-loving Alexandrian of the type dear to Cavafy is to preserve through memory, untouched by doubt or alien influence, the life of passion which he has lost. On the contrary, Cavafy leaves us with the dreadful emotional drama of the lover unresolved, but the seeds of the annihilation of the 'lost passionate life' inescapably planted.

In this poem, then, the opposition between Christianity and paganism is a symbol of the exclusion and alienation of the lover from the beloved's family and environment, and hence, ultimately, from the beloved himself. The fact that the action is set in the dying years of paganism emphasises that the lover is the loser. By the end of the poem the loss of present and future becomes also the threat of loss of the past, as doubt about 'knowledge' of the beloved is induced by the alien context of Christian funeral ritual. And the loss of the past becomes a threat to the lover's sense of his own identity: he is becoming a stranger to Myres, and therefore to his own past self. Cavafy shows us both the importance of memory and the susceptibility of even memory to the physical world. Can we know another person? How do we 'possess' him or her? What forces can destroy that possession? Nor is there any guarantee that the flight at the end will 'preserve the memory of Myres'. For the poem is indeed a double drama: the drama of the experience of alienation, and the drama of re-living it at the moment of re-telling.